PICKLEBALL POINTERS
A PLAYER'S GUIDE TO IMPROVING YOUR SKILLS

BY
Ron Elbe

Written and published by Ronald E. Elbe

First Edition

Copyright © 2018 by Ronald E. Elbe

Printed in the United States of America

All rights reserved. No part of this book may be reproduced or transmitted in any form or by any means, electronic or mechanical including photocopying, recording, or by any information storage or retrieval system, without the written permission of the publisher.

ISBN: 978-1720286615

CONTENTS

DEDICATION & INTRODUCTION 1

    ABOUT THE AUTHOR 2

    DEDICATION 4

    ACKNOWLEDGEMENTS 4

    INTRODUCTION 5

SECTION I --- THE GAME 9

    USAPA RULES 10

    BEFORE THE FIRST SERVE 12

    IT'S A VERY SIMPLE GAME 14

    THE FOUR COMMANDMENTS 16

    CONFLICTING GUIDANCE 20

    WORSE THAN, EQUAL TO, OR BETTER THAN 21

    WATCH AND LEARN 23

SHOOT, MOVE, COMMUNICATE 26

SKINNY SINGLES 30

THE COACH - PLAYER RELATIONSHIP 33

BUT IT WON'T HELP! 37

MISTAKES.. 39

TOURNAMENT PLAY 41

SOURCES AND RESOURCES 45

SECTION II --- EQUIPMENT 48

EQUIPMENT OVERVIEW 49

SECTION III --- PHYSICAL ASPECTS 56

GET A GRIP 57

EFFECTIVE SERVING 59

IF YOU WERE A PITCHER.. 61

COURT POSITION --- 67

MAKING HARD SHOTS LOOK EASY 67

KEEP YOUR EYE ON THE BALL 69

PERIPHERAL VISION 71

THREE STROKES 74

DOING WHAT COMES NATURALLY 76

INTO THE VALLEY OF DEATH 78

WINNING IS ONLY A STEP AWAY 81

YOU'RE NOT TOO SLOW 83

IT'S ALL NEWTON'S FAULT 85

YOU SHOULD BE IN THE MOVIES 87

GAMES VERSUS DRILLS 88

SECTION IV --- MENTAL ASPECTS 92

ELEVEN IS A SMALL NUMBER 93

PLAYING WITH A PURPOSE 94

REACTIVE, ACTIVE, OR PROACTIVE? 98

PICKLEBALL --- THE MENTAL GAME 100

A DICHOTOMY? 102

THE ZONE 106

NOTABLE QUOTES 110

MY PHILOSOPHICAL EVOLUTION 114

RECREATIONAL PLAY VS. TOURNAMENT PLAY 116

ZEN AND THE ART OF PICKLEBALL 118

P A T I E N C E 119

GOOD DAYS AND BAD DAYS 120

WHEN YOU'RE HAVING A BAD DAY 123

BACKSLIDING 125

SEVERAL GREAT SHOTS AND .... A MISS! 127

SPECTATING 129

FEET FETISH 132

IMPORTANT RALLIES 135

SECTION V --- TEAMWORK 137

TEAMWORK 138

THE GOSPEL OF TEAMWORK 139

THE GOSPEL OF COMMUNICATION 141

BASIC AND ADVANCED COMMUNICATIONS 142

I WANNA BOP WITH YOU, BABY 147

IF YOU AIN'T RUBBIN'..153

SECTION VI --- TACTICS 155

THE GOSPEL OF TACTICS 156

CONTROL FREAK!!! 160

NEVER FIGHT FAIR 162

BEATING OPPONENTS WHO ARE BETTER THAN YOU ..164

BEATING THE BANGERS 166

ONLY FOOLS RUSH IN...169

CHAMELEONS 171

LOCATION, LOCATION, LOCATION 174

AT 'EM OR AROUND 'EM..177

LET IT GO!!!!!!!!!!!!!!!!!!!!!!! 181

AFTER A GREAT SAVE............. 184

WHAT'S YOUR TARGET? 185

OFFENSE OR DEFENSE? 187

TO LOB, OR NOT TO LOB, THAT IS THE QUESTION 189

PICK A PAIR 193

IF YOU'RE DRAWN OFF THE COURT 196

IF YOU DO WHAT YOU ALWAYS DID............................. 199

PREDICTABILITY 201

THOUGHTS ON STACKING 203

TIMEOUTS 205

SECTION VII --- EXTERNAL FACTORS 207

ASYMMETRICAL CONDITIONS 208

THE ENEMY OF MY ENEMY IS MY FRIEND 211

SECTION VIII --- SINGLES STRATEGY 215

SINGLES VERSUS DOUBLES STRATEGY 216

THE END 221

DEDICATION & INTRODUCTION

ABOUT THE AUTHOR

At Ron Elbe's high school sports award banquet, Ron's tennis coach said of him: "Ron Elbe is the very best no-talent tennis player I've ever seen." Ron took his coach's statement as a compliment.

At a young age, Ron realized that he would never be as strong, as fast, as coordinated, or as talented as some of his friends. But he loved all kinds of competition. He recognized that, to win, he'd have to practice harder, play harder, and become a true student of any game he attempted.

Throughout the years, Ron has competed in many formal activities, including tennis, football, baseball, softball, table tennis, shuffleboard, archery, rifle shooting, pistol shooting, paintball, and pickleball. Ron's coach's words have rung true in every sport he's attempted. To win, Ron has had to study the game, practice hard, and play hard.

In this book, Ron has attempted to share with you a set of pickleball pointers that go beyond the guidance found in most books and videos. That is not to say that this book is only for the most skilled players. Rather, the book goes into more depth on selected, key topics that are valuable to players at every level.

DEDICATION

These Pointers are dedicated to Jeanie and Chuck Golliher, my sister and brother-in-law, who first introduced me to this wonderful sport at the many beautiful indoor venues around Cocoa Beach, Florida.

ACKNOWLEDGEMENTS

Many people know that Janette Harrington is a very accomplished pickleball player. Few know that she is also an amazing editor and proofreader.
Thank you, Janette.

Brooke Williams, an author published many times over, provided valuable guidance regarding publication and marketing of this book.
Thank you, Brooke.

INTRODUCTION

These Pointers are not intended to be a comprehensive manual about pickleball. There are already many basic resources available. And, I've made a conscious effort to avoid merely rewording knowledge commonly available from a variety of other sources.

Rather, I hope that these Pointers supplement your other resources with additional, valuable points of information that may not be adequately addressed in other sources. Hopefully, all players from new players to experienced students of the game will find worthwhile, new information herein.

I've intentionally kept each Pointer concise. Each is typically one or two pages long. Each focuses on only one specific topic. I've attempted to use language that will make the text easy to understand, easy to remember, and easy to implement.

To make it easy for you to find topics of interest, I've divided the Pointers into eight Sections:

    I. The Game
    II. Equipment

III. Physical Aspects
IV. Mental Aspects
V. Teamwork
VI. Tactics
VII. External Factors
VIII. Singles Strategy

If you've never played pickleball, it's certainly possible to find a venue, walk in and ask someone to show you how to play. Most recreational players are happy to help a "newbie". Without more research or study, you can probably pick up enough basics of the game to have a great time just playing for the fun of it.

But, if you're competitive, you'll want to improve ...... to learn how to play the game better ...... to learn how to play it correctly. That improvement will require study, research, and practice beyond what you'll find at most recreational venues.

As with almost any subject, the most comprehensive source of information is the internet. Books are good, but they are limited in scope. And some topics are much easier to grasp visually than by reading. So I've included references to numerous sources of valuable information, particularly YouTube videos. If you search each of those sources and study them, you will find much additional valuable information.

Pickleball is most popularly played as Doubles. Consequently, the Pointers are discussed primarily in terms of the Doubles game. However, most of the Pointers are also applicable to Singles. And I've included a separate section on the subject of Singles Strategy.

As you read these Pointers, you may notice that some topics are discussed in more than one Pointer. That redundancy isn't an accident. My feeling is that if I address an important topic in more than one way, at least one of the Pointers may strike a chord with you.

I would urge you not to think of this book as a training manual to be read from front to back, implementing each chapter as you go. Rather think of the Pointers as a series of concise notes (or emails if you prefer) from me to you on specific topics. Think of each Pointer as an individual note to you, each of which is intended to assist you on one specific facet of your game.

I'd suggest that you read the book once in its entirety to familiarize yourself with the contents of each Pointer. After you've read the book, you can use the index to locate an individual topic that is of immediate concern to you right now, and read my Pointers to you on that topic. Think of this book as a reference library where you can repeatedly go to find knowledge and reminders on specific topics of immediate interest to you.

IMPORTANT NOTE: Reading these Pointers will be of ABSOLUTELY NO VALUE to your game unless you IMPLEMENT THEIR TEACHINGS on the court.

(We all know that both men and women play this game we love. These Pointers are certainly intended to help both genders become better players. But, I'm not going to write "him/her" everywhere, so please don't be offended at my failure to write both genders.

These Pointers began as a series of notes I emailed to my pickleball friends. But the number of topics that I wanted to share rapidly grew to a point where they needed some organization. Thus this book was born.

Ron

SECTION I --- THE GAME

Pickleball Pointers

USAPA RULES

The USA Pickleball Association is the governing body for organized pickleball in the United States. The USAPA establishes and updates the rules of the game.

Those rules include specifications for balls and paddles. So, USAPA also tests and approves/disapproves every make and model of paddle that manufacturers want to have approved for USAPA tournament play.

As with nearly all organizations these days, USAPA has a website. If you search "USAPA Pickleball" on the internet, it should pop right up.

I'd suggest that you peruse the entire USAPA website thoroughly. It has lots of useful information.

Pickleball is still an evolving sport. Consequently, USAPA's rules are evolving too.

Section I --- The Game

It would be worthwhile for you to review the current USAPA rules if you haven't done so recently. Just look under "Rules & Referees" on the USAPA website.

Ron

Pickleball Pointers

BEFORE THE FIRST SERVE

Have you ever noticed that your first and last games of the day tend to be your worst? I have. I thought about this phenomenon. I concluded that my first game was poor because I wasn't yet fully mentally focused on pickleball. I still had residual thoughts of other topics on my mind. And I concluded that my last game was poor because I was physically worn out.

To improve my first game, I've started to mentally think about pickleball as I drive to the courts. I set goals for the day and visualize specific shots. (Yeah, I know that I still have to drive safely. I can do both simultaneously.) I continue to sharpen my mental focus as I warm up. By the time of the first serve, I'm focused.

As I warm up, I try to hit a wide variety of my shots. I'm practicing all of my shots and simultaneously watching my opponents to see which of my shots are difficult for them to return. Those are the shots I'll hit at them in the game.

To improve my last game, I make certain that I get enough rest the night before, and eat light, but healthy before I go to the courts, and I take a granola snack with me. Dehydration can also cause physical weakness. My 40 ounce thermos is always full of ice water.

After I get to the courts, I take the time to stretch and fully loosen up before I play. Far too many players arrive, walk onto the court immediately, hit a half-dozen dinks, and declare that they are ready to play. I think not. I think they aren't loose enough to play their best. They are risking muscular injuries.

The mental and physical changes I've made to my "before the first serve" routine have made all my games better, especially my first and last ones.

Ron

IT'S A VERY SIMPLE GAME

Tactically, pickleball is a very simple game. In fact, we can summarize the tactics in only two rules (each of which has three corollaries).

I. **THE TEAM THAT MAKES THE FEWEST UNFORCED ERRORS WINS.**

    1. Five mortal sins:

        --Missing a serve;

        --Missing a serve return;

        -- Hitting a poor 3rd shot;

        --Overhitting a setup;

        --Both (or neither) team members going for a shot.

    2. The team that communicates and moves together the best wins.

    3. The team that forces its opponents into disadvantageous tactical positions while maintaining good tactical positions themselves wins.

II. **THE TEAM THAT HITS BALLS DOWNWARD WHILE FORCING THEIR OPPONENTS TO HIT BALLS UPWARDS WINS.**

Section I --- The Game

1. The team that first gets both players SAFELY to the Non Volley Zone wins.
2. The team that makes third shot drops consistently wins.
3. The team that dinks best wins.

Ron

Pickleball Pointers

THE FOUR COMMANDMENTS

There are Four Commandments in Pickleball. They are:

I. MINIMIZE THY UNFORCED ERRORS
1. Don't miss routine shots.
2. Move quickly to get into position early to make shots. Then stop before you hit the ball. Avoid hitting shots while you are moving. That will make more shots routine.

II. HIE THEE TO THE NON VOLLEY ZONE
1. At the start of every rally, your first goal should be to hit shots that allow you and your partner to get safely to your NVZ.
2. Hitting high, deep shots will give you more time to get to your NVZ.
3. Once you get to the NVZ, there are only two reasons you should back up.
    a. Your opponent hits a lob that you must go back to hit.
    b. You or your partner hits such a poor lob that it will be smashed back at you.

4. If you do get driven back from your NVZ, hit shots that will allow you to regain your NVZ ASAP.

III. DIRECT THY SHOTS TOWARD THY OPPONENTS FEET
1. As long as you keep your opponents back from their NVZ, it should be easy to hit balls at their feet. If your opponents get to their NVZ, you'll need to dink them.

IV. PLAY AS A TEAM WITH THY PARTNER
1. Communication is critical and it's easy. It's a very simple language with only five basic phrases------- Mine, Yours, Out, Bounce It, and Switch. It's amazing that 99% of players do far too little communicating.
2. Move up, back, and laterally together.

Essentially everything taught by good instructors is in support of one or more of the above commandments. When you're taking a clinic or just doing drills, try to relate what you are doing to these commandments.

When you are playing a game, if you only remember these Four Commandments, you should do well.

If you are playing against knowledgeable opponents, they will also be attempting to follow the Four Commandments. As you follow these Four Commandments, you also want to force your opponents to violate them.

Force your opponents to violate the Four Commandments by:

I. GIVE THY OPPONENTS LOTS OF OPPORTUNITIES TO MAKE UNFORCED ERRORS

1. Keep the ball in play. Give your opponents lots and lots of opportunities to make unforced errors.
2. Avoid hitting shots that your opponents can easily slam for a winner. That doesn't qualify as keeping the ball in play.
3. Hit shots that force your opponents to move. It will be harder for them to hit good shots if they are moving.

II. KEEP THY OPPONENTS BACK FROM THE NON VOLLEY ZONE

1. If your opponents are both back, hit deep shots at their feet, intending to keep them back.
2. If one of your opponents is back and the other is up at the NVZ, pick on the opponent who is back. Only hit the ball at the opponent who is up if you can hit the ball hard enough to defeat his reflexes.

III. FORCE THY OPPONENTS TO HIT HIGH SHOTS

1. As long as you keep your opponents back from their NVZ, you should easily be able to hit shots at their feet, forcing them to hit difficult, upward shots.
2. If both of your opponents reach their NVZ, you will need to dink them in order to keep your shots at their feet. Just keep drinking them until they make a mistake and hit a high shot that you can return for a winner.

IV. MAKE IT DIFFICULT FOR THY OPPONENTS TO PLAY AS A TEAM

1. Most teams don't move up and back together. Hit your shots at the back player, keeping him back so that they can't get together.
2. Most teams don't move laterally together. Try to hit shots that draw one opponent wide to his side of the court. His partner probably won't slide to the middle of the court to cover. That will leave you an open half court to hit a winner into.

Ron

Pickleball Pointers

CONFLICTING GUIDANCE

As you continue to evolve your game, you will probably receive guidance, counsel, and opinions about your game from coaches, players, clinics, and videos. Some of this guidance simply won't make sense. Other guidance will be conflicting. How can you sort it out?

I'd suggest two ways.

First you can try it all and see what works for you. That's not a bad process.
Just remember, things that work for other players may not work for you.
And there are many players (and some coaches) who dispense advice that isn't particularly good.

Second, you can eliminate some poor guidance without trying it by seeing whether it supports our Four Commandments. If it violates any of those commandments and their corollaries, I doubt if it is worthy of your consideration.

Section I --- The Game

WORSE THAN, EQUAL TO, OR BETTER THAN

Every time you and your partner step on the court, you will face opponents who are worse than you, about equal to you, or better than you.

Each type of opponent is a different learning opportunity. To improve your play, you need to understand and take advantage of all those learning opportunities.

OPPONENTS WORSE THAN YOU PROVIDE OPPORTUNITIES TO:
-- Practice shots that need improvement.
-- Practice intently, focusing on seeing your paddle hit the ball every time.
-- Practice getting stopped and into the proper position before every shot you hit.
-- Practice stacking.
-- Practice playing under calm mental control.
-- Practice your communication skills and teamwork.
-- Test and develop new shots and tactics.

OPPONENTS EQUAL TO YOU PROVIDE OPPORTUNITIES TO:

-- Play long, close games that develop your mental and physical toughness.

-- Learn that pickleball is a game of streaks where, if you play hard continuously and focus intently, you can come from far behind to win. On the other hand, if you ease up or lose focus, your opponents may come from far behind.

-- Practice, against good opponents, the skills you developed against inferior opponents.

OPPONENTS BETTER THAN YOU PROVIDE OPPORTUNITIES TO:

-- Test the limits of your skills.

-- Learn to accept defeat graciously.

-- Work hard on minimizing the weaknesses that your good opponents expose.

-- Be exposed to opponent's advanced shots, skills, and tactics that you need to develop.

Don't waste any learning opportunities. Recognize the learning opportunities that each type of opponent offers and focus your game to take advantage of those opportunities.

Ron

Section I --- The Game

WATCH AND LEARN

You can improve your pickleball skills a great deal without being on a court.

When you're sitting on the sidelines waiting to play, you can do one of three things.

    1. You can socialize.

    2. You can watch the ongoing games for their entertainment value.

    3. You can study the ongoing games to improve your skills.

If you choose to do either of the first two options, I can't help you. But if you choose to do the third, I have a few thoughts that may be helpful.

As you study ongoing games, you can observe the flow of each rally to understand why it was won or lost. Then you can avoid the mistakes that caused the losses and adopt the strengths that won the rallies.

You can also observe individual players to learn their strengths and weaknesses. Then you'll be better prepared to avoid their strengths and focus on their weaknesses when you play against them.

You can also learn a great deal by studying pickleball matches on YouTube.

One video that I found particularly instructive isn't just one match. Rather, it's a compilation of great rallies from a number of matches. You might also find it instructive. Just internet search "Encinitas Pickleball Rec Play November 2016".

Regardless of what match you are watching on YouTube, watch it once just for the fun of watching.

Watch it a second time, picking out one player and concentrating on watching him (rather than just watching the ball go back and forth). Study how he plays each shot. Look for his strengths and weaknesses. Remember them. When you play, emulate his strengths and avoid his weaknesses. Study how he and his partner work together. (It really is almost like a dance.)

Watch it a third time. This time watch:
-- How smoothly the players play. It's almost like they are playing in slow motion. They never seem rushed.

Section I --- The Game

-- How effectively they use offensive lobs.

-- How they hit winners AROUND the net when a dink draws them off the court.

-- How they move as a team, up/back and side to side as the flow of the play dictates.

-- How they communicate.

-- How well they hit spots.

-- How they move dinks back and forth against their opponents to create an opening that they can exploit.

-- How they follow through on each shot, even dinks.

-- How they anticipate the opponent's shot in order to be in the optimum position.

-- How they always return immediately to their ready position after each shot.

Ron

Pickleball Pointers

SHOOT, MOVE, COMMUNICATE

If I said "Our goal is to bend the opposition to our will, to place him in a disadvantageous position, and to defeat him." would I be talking about a U.S. Military operation or a pickleball match?

The correct answer to that question is "Both." While pickleball is certainly not a life or death matter, it is a competition which we want to win. And some of the skills taught to the military are applicable to pickleball. Three of those key, transferable skills are to Shoot, Move, and Communicate.

SHOOT

The most obvious pickleball skill is hitting the ball. (It is analogous to "shooting".) The better our target selection and the more accurate our hitting, the better our chances of placing our opponents in a disadvantageous position and defeating them. Practice and play with a goal of improving your accuracy. If you can hit the serve into the opponent's service court every time, then try to hit a selected portion of the court. Do that with every shot. Keep focusing on, and hitting, smaller and smaller target areas.

MOVE

Most players move too late and too little. Move to the most likely spot you'll need to be in before your opponent even hits his shot. Adjust your location as he hits the shot.

Never reach for a shot if you have time to move to it and hit it strongly. Each time you reach for a shot, ask yourself if you had time to take a step instead of reaching to hit the ball strongly instead of awkwardly.

Every shot during a rally may necessitate your moving to be in the optimum position on the court.

COMMUNICATE

Perhaps the most famous line in the classic movie, "Cool Hand Luke" is: "What we have here is a failure to communicate."

Of the three skills, Shoot, Move, and Communicate, the least developed skill in most players is communication.

Time after time, we can watch both partners go after the same ball (or worse, neither goes after a ball). Time after time, we can watch a player try to return a lob that was obviously going out because he was looking up and his partner didn't call it out for him. Time after time, we see both partners end up on the same side of the court because neither one called "Switch". Etc. etc. etc. etc.

Good pickleball partners have evolved a standardized set of shorthand words and phrases to communicate with each other.

Here's a list of the most basic and their meanings:

MINE -------------- I will take the shot.

YOURS ------------ You hit the shot.

OUT --------------- I believe that the ball will land out. Don't hit it.

IN ------------------ I believe that the ball will land in. Hit it.

BOUNCE IT ------ I'm uncertain whether the ball will land in or out. Let it bounce before you hit it.

UP ---------------- Move forward to the NVZ.

BACK -------------- Move backward to the baseline.

SWITCH ---------- Change sides of the court.

NOW (or GO) --- The situation is right to hit a winner. Go for it.

But what do you do if you have a partner who doesn't/won't communicate with you? In that case, you'll have to redouble your efforts to communicate with him. You can also talk to him about communication before the game and between rallies, encouraging him to communicate.

Remember, it is impossible to communicate too much. Get in the habit of communicating all of the time, not just when you think it is crucial to do so.

Pickleball Pointers

SKINNY SINGLES

A really good transition from drills to playing games is playing Skinny Singles. In case you're not familiar with Skinny Singles, let me explain.

Skinny Singles is, as the name implies, a singles match with only one player on each side of the net. But, rather than using the whole court, in Skinny Singles, only one half of the court is in play. The two players agree to use either the left or right half of the court. Any ball hit to the other side of the court is OUT. Yeah, I know there isn't any line that divides the left and right halves of the NVZ. So players just have to guesstimate that line.

Obviously, if you play on only one side of the court, service can't be done diagonally across the court. Service is directly ahead. (But you could play diagonally if you want to.)

There's only one player on a team so service changes to the receiving player each time a rally is lost by the server. Scoring is simplified too. Because there's only one server on each side, there's no need to call Server 1 or Server 2. Games are played to 11 points, win by 2, just like an ordinary game.

Section I --- The Game

A quick search of "Skinny Singles Pickleball" will provide you with lots of detailed information on it.

OK, now that we understand the game, let's talk about why Skinny Singles is such a valuable learning tool.

First, you're under no pressure to hit your comfortable shots to avoid risking the wrath of your partner. You can hit shots that you usually aren't comfortable hitting.

Second, it is a competitive game with some attendant adrenaline (not just a boring drill). It's a fun learning tool.

Third, since it's not an "official" game, you and your opponent can make up rules that allow you both to practice skills that you want to upgrade. For example, let's say that you both want to work on your third shot drops. You two can agree that if the third shot doesn't drop into the NVZ, the server loses the rally. Or, if you want to work on your dinking, you can agree that once both of you reach the NVZ, you both must dink until someone misses. Or, if you want to work on your finesse game, you can agree that no slams are allowed. Or………………………

Pickleball Pointers

Fourth, without a partner, you hit EVERY shot that comes to your side of the net. You get LOTS of practice in a short period of time.

Fifth, you must constantly be mentally into the game. You have no partner to cover for your mental lapses.

Sixth, the smaller width of the playing area forces you to make accurate shots.

A good approach to a morning's play is to practice a particular drill (or two or three) for ten to fifteen minutes. Then incorporate those drills as rules into thirty minutes of Skinny Singles.

If you arrive at the courts early, you may find empty courts and one or two players standing around waiting for other players to arrive. This is a great opportunity to play skinny singles with one of them.

I think you'll be surprised at how quickly your skills will improve. And, you'll get to play fun, competitive games as you improve.

Ron

Section I --- The Game

THE COACH - PLAYER RELATIONSHIP

If you seriously desire to improve your game, sooner or later you'll obtain the services of a coach. That coach may be someone who puts on formal clinics, or it may be a personal professional coach, or it may just be a skilled player. To learn the most you can from a coach, it's important to understand the coach-player relationship. There are three types of coach-player relationships.

PROFESSIONAL COACH AND PROFESSIONAL PLAYER

The professional coach of a professional player has a financial interest in the player's performance. The occupation of the coach and the occupation of the player are intertwined. Their salaries are interdependent.

Often they have a long-term relationship.

Because of their financial interrelationship, the coach expects/demands that the player incorporate the coach's direction into the player's play.

PROFESSIONAL COACH AND AMATEUR PLAYER

The professional coach of an amateur player is paid to give his best effort to assure that the player understands coach's guidance and counsel.

The coach is paid, therefore he is expected to be knowledgeable and correct in his guidance.

The player is an amateur. He isn't receiving a salary for his play. So the salaries of the coach and player are not intertwined.

The relationship may be either short term or long term.

The coach is not normally held responsible for subsequent player performance.

The coach offers guidance and counsel which the player may, or may not, implement.

AMATEUR COACH AND AMATEUR PLAYER

The coach is not paid, therefore he has no obligation to be correct and knowledgeable in his guidance. His coaching is strictly a "best effort" exercise.

The relationship may be either short term or long term.

The coach has no responsibility for subsequent player performance.

The coach offers guidance and counsel which the player may, or may not, implement.

Section I --- The Game

Now that you know what to expect from a coach, let me share my personal philosophy about coaching.

MY PERSONAL PHILOSOPHY ABOUT COACHING

When I need guidance, counsel, or support, I seek out the best "coach" I can find. I listen closely to his guidance. I ask all of the pertinent questions that I can think of. I reiterate his teachings back to him so that I am certain that I understand them correctly.

Then, I FOLLOW MY COACH'S GUIDANCE EXPLICITELY! (I follow this philosophy regardless of whether my "coach" is a doctor, dentist, accountant, financial counselor, a sports coach, or other person, paid or unpaid.)

I select my coaches because I believe they are more skilled, knowledgeable and/or experienced than I am. If I've spent the effort to find the most knowledgeable "coach" that I can, it would indeed be foolish to disregard his guidance.

I simply do not understand people who hire professionals to support them and then ignore the professional's advice. That's just dumb. Such people waste their money and their time as well as the time of their coach.

Likewise, when someone asks me for guidance, I would hope that they would accept and implement that guidance. If not, they have simply wasted my time and theirs.

Ron

Section I --- The Game

BUT IT WON'T HELP!

If you want to improve your game:

--You could watch lots of YouTube videos.

But it won't help.

--You could read a number of pickleball books.

But it won't help.

-- You could go to clinics.

But it won't help.

--You could find a coach or mentor to teach you.

But it won't help.

None of these things, in and of themselves, will help. The most they can do is provide you with knowledge of how to improve your game. Only implementing that knowledge on the court will improve your game.

Unfortunately, practicing new skills and new shots may temporarily lower the level of your play. It has been my observation that most players won't make the necessary sacrifices. They want to win NOW, even if it means they won't improve.

Pickleball Pointers

If you are willing to forego a few current wins to improve your game in the long term, the solution is simple. You must learn from videos, books, clinics, and coaches. Then you must implement that knowledge every shot of every rally of every game until it becomes automatic. Obviously you can't implement, all at once, everything you learn. You need to focus on one important improvement that you believe will significantly improve your play and practice it every shot of every rally of every game. When that improvement is a normal part of every game, then move on to another improvement.

Let me add one encouraging thought. If you choose to make the sacrifices necessary to improve, you will be one of the few players who do. Most of your competitors won't be improving. In the long term, you'll beat them more easily and more frequently.

Ron

Section I --- The Game

MISTAKES

I have some good news for you.

Right now your best shots are probably good enough to play at the 4.5 or 5.0 level. And your good shots are good enough to play at a higher level than you are currently playing.
So what's holding you back?
It's mistakes.
As you play against better and better players, the penalty for mistakes is higher and comes far more swiftly.
At the 3.0 level and below, you can make several mistakes during a rally and still have a chance to win it.
At the 3.5 and 4.0 levels, you might get away with one mistake in a rally or, if you are lucky, two.
At the 4.5 and 5.0 levels, if you make a mistake you will pay immediately and decisively.

    --- If you hit a short lob, you'll eat it.

    --- If you hit a high dink, you'll wear it.

    --- If you hit a shot that's going out, your opponents won't save you by hitting it.

    --- If you fail to get to the kitchen, you'll be dancing around a ball at your feet.

--- If you get caught out of position, you'll see your opponent's winner zing past.

--- If you fail to work as a team with your partner, the gaps between and around your team will be filled with winning shots.

--- If you fail to communicate with your partner, your opponents will make you feel lonely indeed.

--- If you fail to focus intently, even for a moment, the rally will be over.

--- If you fail to hit a winner when given the opportunity, you won't get another chance.

--- If you have any weaknesses in your physical or mental game that cause you to make mistakes, your opponents will exploit them unmercifully.

If you want to improve your play......if you want to compete successfully at higher levels......don't spend time trying to learn to hit more great shots.

Rather, work on reducing the number of mistakes you make.

Far, far more rallies are lost by mistakes than are won by great shots.

Ron

Section I --- The Game

TOURNAMENT PLAY

Recreational play is fun. But, tournament play adds a whole new level of intensity (and adrenaline) to the game. I certainly recommend that you play in a few tournaments to assess them for yourself.

TYPES OF TOURNAMENTS

Tournaments can be divided into two types based on how they rank the participants. Some tournaments segregate players based on the age of the youngest team member. Other tournaments segregate players based on the highest USAPA skill ranking of a team member.

Most tournaments will have sub-tournaments for men's doubles, ladies' doubles, and mixed doubles. Some tournaments also have men's singles and ladies' singles matches. Usually, you are allowed to enter any, or all of them.

In most tournaments, you will have dedicated partners. But in some tournaments (called "ladder" or "mixer" tournaments), you are randomly assigned a different partner for each game.

RATING YOURSELF

In most skill-segregated tournaments, you rate yourself based on numerical USAPA guidelines. USAPA uses a numerical ranking system that starts at 1.0 (for a complete novice) and goes up in 0.5 increments to 5.0 (highest amateur status).

On the USAPA website, look under "Tournaments & Ratings".

Skill-segregated tournaments that rely on self-rating have an obvious weakness. Players who want to win rate themselves low. I've seen players rate themselves as 3.0 when they display all of the skills that USAPA describes for 4.0 or even 4.5.

There seems to be a large tournament-to-tournament disparity in self-rating too. I've watched 3.0, 3.5, 4.0 and 4.5 matches on YouTube. I've seen many 3.0 matches where the players were far more advanced than 4.0 players in other tournaments.

My advice would be to rate yourself conservatively in your first tournament. After a tournament or two, you'll be able to ascertain how you should rate yourself in relation to the other players in your area.

Remember, you can certainly rate yourself low in order to win. But it's really no fun beating up on inferior players. Try to rate yourself so that you challenge your skills.

PICKING A PARTNER

If you're in a tournament that segregates players based on age, you'll probably want to pick a partner similar in age to you. Remember, your team will be categorized based on the age of the YOUNGEST player. If you are 70 and your partner is 50, you'll be playing against 50 year old teams.

Likewise, if you're in a tournament that segregates players based on skill, you'll probably want to pick a partner similar in skill level to you. Your team will be categorized based on the highest skill level. If you're a 3.0 and your partner is a 4.5, you'll be playing 4.5 teams all day long!

I like to pick a partner whose style compliments mine. I'm a soft player. I have bad shoulders, so I'm not a hard slammer. I like dink shots and angle shots. I prefer a partner who can put away a vicious slam. I set him up with dinks and angles. He gets the glory of hitting the winners. Most of all, I want a partner who's fun to be with on the court. One who supports me. One that I can support. One who believes that pickleball is a TEAM sport. One who has fun regardless of whether we win or lose.

FINDING A TOURNAMENT

The USAPA website is a wealth of information. It lists many of the major tournaments. Just look under "Tournaments & Ratings" on the USAPA home page. Many large and small tournaments use "pickleballtournaments.com" to publicize their tournaments. Many Senior Olympics organizations around the country now include pickleball as one of their sports. Be sure to check Senior Olympics websites around your area.

Finding tournaments is another good reason for joining a pickleball club if there's one in your area. They keep track of all local and some national tournaments.

Ron

Section I --- The Game

SOURCES AND RESOURCES

The sources and resources that I discuss in this section are not intended to be a comprehensive list. They are simply a sample of the sources and resources available to you if you put forth even a modicum of effort to search for them.

EQUIPMENT

A number of on-line companies, including Amazon and several pickleball-specific companies, supply equipment to our sport. The only on-line retailer that I have purchased from is Pickleball Central. In my experience, Pickleball Central is a really great internet company. Their guidance on paddles is very interesting, as are the customer reviews of all of their products. I'm sure many other companies are good too. I just don't have any personal experience with them.

Some brick-and-mortar sporting goods retailers also carry pickleball equipment. Dick's Sporting Goods is one example. However, their selection will be limited and their staff probably won't be of much technical assistance to you.

PLACES TO PLAY

Pickleball courts aren't scattered uniformly across the U.S. Some communities have very active clubs and multiple indoor and outdoor venues. Other communities (even highly urbanized communities) have few players and practically no venues. There are several ways to find venues in any given metropolitan area.

The USAPA website has a whole section entitled "Places To Play". It contains lists of clubs, and a map that shows the locations of thousands of courts across the U.S. Just look on the USAPA Home Page for the tab entitled "Places To Play".

Call your local Parks and Recreation Departments and Tennis Clubs. They will likely be knowledgeable.

As you look for places to play, be aware that some outdoor venues have dedicated pickleball courts. They are designed for nothing else. Other outdoor venues and practically all indoor venues have multi-use courts that are sized and lined for tennis, basketball, volleyball, etc. as well as pickleball. The many superfluous lines on multi-use courts may make the boundaries of the pickleball court hard to identify during the heat of a rally. That's one reason I prefer to play outdoors on dedicated pickleball courts.

KNOWLEDGE

There are many, many pickleball instructional videos and pickleball matches on YouTube. Just search "pickleball" and then hit "videos". Watching them is a quick and easy way to learn the sport.

The "Pickleball Channel" has good instructional videos in their Pickleball 411 section, as does "Betterpickleball.com".

I really like "Third Shot Sports" pickleball instructional videos by Mark Renneson. They aren't long, but they are very well done on specific topics. I also like Joe Baker's videos. Just search for Joe Baker Pickleball

YouTube has literally hundreds of matches. I'd suggest that you watch a few every night. And try to watch a variety of skill levels as well as mens', womens', and co-ed games.

There are a number of other interesting pickleball websites including "Pickleballx.com", and "Pickleballinstructions.com". Spend a little time searching the internet. It will be well worth your time.

SECTION II --- EQUIPMENT

Section II --- Equipment

EQUIPMENT OVERVIEW

USAPA

USAPA recognizes that the very nature of the game can be greatly altered by advances in equipment. Paddles that impart more spin, or allow higher ball speeds, or balls that bounce much higher or lower, etc., can destroy the game as we love and play it now. So, USAPA has developed strict standards for both balls and paddles. Each model of paddle and ball must be tested and approved by USAPA before it can be used in sanctioned tournaments. I'd suggest that, even if you don't plan to play in tournaments, you select your paddle and balls from among the approved lists on the USAPA website.

The list of approved paddles and balls can be found under "Rules & Referees" on the USAPA website. In case you're inquisitive, the specific tests for paddles and balls are defined in Section 2 of the USAPA Rule Book which you can also find under "Rules and Referees".

PADDLES

Common advice for new players is to play with as many paddles as possible. Then buy the one you like best. In actuality, I don't believe that most new players can tell one paddle from another. It probably takes six months to a year of experience before their game reaches a level of sophistication that will allow them to select a paddle. When you get to be a solid 3.0 to 3.5 player, you're ready to start the search for your perfect paddle.

I'd suggest that new players merely go on a website such as Pickleball Central, read their guidance and customer reviews of the more popular paddles. Then just buy a paddle and play. But, I don't ever recommend one of the cheap, wooden paddles. Buy at least a mid-priced paddle.

Unless you are unusually big or small, a mid-weight paddle (7.5 To 8.0 ounces) with a medium sized handle (4.0 to 4.25 inches in diameter) is probably appropriate. Women typically do better with lighter paddles (7.2-7.5 ounces) and a small grip.

In terms of grip size, it's always wise to select the smaller grip. For a few dollars, you can buy an overgrip to increase the size of the paddles' grip. There isn't any handy way to reduce the size of the grip. Also, speaking of grips, I like a grip that is more oblong (rather than round) in cross section. I can feel the angle of the paddle in my hand better with an oblong grip.

My favorite paddle is a 7.6 to 7.8 ounce Engage Encore. It fits my style of play and my hand well.

TOURNA-GRIP

Tourna-Grip is a thin blue non-adhesive wrap for tennis racquet and pickleball paddle grips. If your grip gets slippery when it's sweaty, Tourna-Grip is the answer. It's inexpensive. It's thin enough that it doesn't alter the size of feel of your grip. It will last for many weeks of hard play before it needs to be replaced. I always carry a roll in my pickleball bag.

BALLS

When you go to a new-to-you venue where others are playing, you'll probably find that the players at that venue have already decided on a model and color of ball. They will probably want to play with the balls that they are familiar with. So, it's doubtful that you will have to provide a ball.

If you want to take balls with you, select a popular model from the approved list. Pick a color that will give you optimum visibility at the venue(s) that you most commonly visit. Customer reviews of pickleballs on Pickleball Central can be helpful in choosing durable, visible, popular brands of pickleballs.

And remember that there are both indoor and outdoor balls. Take the kind that's appropriate for the venue you'll be visiting.

ATTIRE

USAPA does have some restrictions on clothing. (You can read those restrictions in the USAPA Rule Book.) But, oddly enough, they do not restrict the color of clothing. You could legally outfit yourself in a color that matches the color of the balls being used. Even though that would be legal, it is considered to be in poor form (as the British would say). If you don't want to be looked down upon by other players, I suggest you don't wear clothing that closely matches ball color.

When I first started playing pickleball, I wore cotton. It only took a few games before I realized that cotton was not appropriate. My cotton clothes got drenched with sweat and stayed that way. I now wear all wicking clothes --- shirt, shorts, undershorts, and socks. I play much cooler and more comfortably now.

I consider a cap or visor an indispensable part of my attire when playing outdoors (and, at some indoor venues). Without one, you'll lose sight of lots of balls that are lobbed up into the sun.

Shoes are such a personal decision that I can't make a recommendation for you. However, I'd note that I have wide feet and the only shoes I can find that fit me are Nike Air Monarch IVs. Court or tennis shoes are often recommended by others, but I simply have no experience with them.

On the subject of shoes --- I always wear my casual shoes very loose. I can step into them without unlacing them. I learned that loose-fitting shoes aren't appropriate for pickleball. Twice I ran right out of a shoe. But that's not the worst of it. When I'd run forward and then make a quick stop, my feet would slide forward in my shoes. My toes got so bruised that they turned black and blue. Now I tie my pickleball shoes so tightly that I have to use a shoe horn to put them on. They fit just fine for pickleball.

WATER BOTTLE

On the average, I lose about five pounds in water weight during a morning's play. I couldn't play without frequent water breaks. I take a double-walled, stainless steel, large-mouthed water bottle with flip top drinking spout. It holds 40 ounces. I put in two 16 ounce bottles of water and then fill it with ice. The water stays ice cold all day long.

SAFETY GLASSES

I've seen two players receive significant eye injuries from pickleballs. I highly recommend that every pickleball player wear glasses. If you don't wear prescription glasses, purchase sports-oriented safety glasses. Truly, you do have only one set of eyes. With only one eye, you'll lack any depth perception. Your playing days will be over.

BIFOCALS

Bifocals suck!!!!

I tried for quite a while to play with bifocals. I found that low balls simply evaporated from my view. I gave up and purchased single-vision prescription glasses specifically for sports, including pickleball. MAJOR IMPROVEMENT!!!!!

GLOVES

Balls aren't the only pickleball-related equipment that can cause an injury. Frequently both teammates swing at the same ball. Sometimes those swings can intersect, causing bruising and laceration of hands and wrists. Such injuries can be avoided by wearing appropriate gloves. Stores that sell tools (Lowes, Menards, etc.), sell gloves with plastic covering the back of the hand and fingers. Look near the wrenches, drills, saws, etc. Those gloves are perfect for protecting hands from swinging paddles.

Section II --- Equipment

(You actually only need to wear one --- on your paddle hand. You can give the other one to a friend who swings from the other side.)

MISCELLANEOUS EQUIPMENT

I also take a towel, glasses cleaning wipes, knee supports (because I'm old and my knees are worn out), granola bars, and some money. I keep all of my pickleball equipment ready to go in a dedicated pickleball bag.

Ron

SECTION III --- PHYSICAL ASPECTS

Section III --- Physical Aspects

__GET A GRIP__

I'm surprised at the number of experienced players who handicap themselves by using an inconsistent and/or suboptimum grip. By that I mean that the paddle isn't in the best angle, rotationally, in their hand.

If you watch for these players, they are fairly easy to identify. Their shots often take off in directions far different than normal. Also look for players who use strange contortions when hitting the ball. Some of them even attempt to hit balls on their backhand side with the forehand side of the paddle. Players who suffer from either or both of these problems, really need to pay attention to how they grip their paddles.

There are two keys to a good grip on your paddle.

First, the paddle face should be vertical when you naturally hold your paddle out to your forehand side and also when you hold your paddle out to your backhand side. The easiest way I've found to explain this grip is the "hammer" analogy.
Grip the paddle as if it were a hammer and you were going to pound in a nail with the edge of the paddle.

Second, your grip on the paddle must be consistent. It must be the same, rotationally, in your hand all of the time.

If you find that you need to improve your grip, you might want to look at it after every rally to insure that it's correct.

I like paddle grips that are oblong in cross-section rather than grips that are roundish in cross section. I can feel the oblong grip so I know that my grip is correct and consistent without looking down.

Ron

Section III --- Physical Aspects

EFFECTIVE SERVING

Some players have difficulty consistently putting their serves in the court.

That's very bad.

Coaches and videos stress the importance of not missing serves. Consequently, many players think of their serve as simply a way to start a rally. They consider any serve they get into the court as a good serve.

That's also bad.

I'd suggest that a good serve is far more than just any serve that hits in the court. Remember, the serving team always starts at a disadvantage. The receiving team already has one player at the kitchen and the serving team must stay back until the second bounce. A good serve will help mitigate the serving team's disadvantage by making it difficult for the receiver to come to the kitchen.

Here is how I would rate serves.

Missed...................Catastrophic

Short and High...........Very poor

Short and Low...................Poor

Deep and Low..........Acceptable

Deep and High.............Excellent

The better the serve, the longer it will keep the receiver back. A deep, high serve will keep the receiver at or behind his baseline until he hits it. At the worst, he will be delayed getting to the kitchen. At the best, he may not come to the kitchen at all. It would be nice to have a variety of serves to keep your opponents guessing. But if you're only going to have one serve, it should be deep and high.

So start thinking about your serve as an offensive weapon, not just as a way to start play.

If you want to improve your serve, there are lots of good training videos on YouTube. As a minimum, check out the following:

"Three Serves & Why You Need Them" in Pickleball Channel's Pickleball 411 section.

"How To Serve Like A Pro", a Third Shot Sports video.

"How To Hit A Consistent Pickleball Serve" on Betterpicklebal.com.

Ron

Section III --- Physical Aspects

IF YOU WERE A PITCHER............

If you were a pitcher who only threw one type of pitch, how effective would you be? Regardless of whether that pitch was a fastball to the center of the strike zone, or a curve ball to the inside half of the strike zone, or a slider outside and low of the strike zone, you'd fare poorly. Batters would soon adapt to your pitch. They would anticipate it and hit it well.

If you were a tennis player who only had one type of serve, how effective would you be?

If you were a football quarterback who only ran the same play time after time, how effective would you be?

It should be clear that having only one pitch, one serve, or one play would cause you to lose a major tactical advantage.

In most sports, the player who initiates the action has the opportunity to vary how he initiates it. He has the ability to prevent his opponent from anticipating, and preparing for, his approach.

Pickleball Pointers

Let me be perfectly clear about this: **The player who first places doubt, hesitation, and uncertainty into the mind of his opponent has a major tactical advantage!**

In pickleball, the server is the first player in each rally to be in a position to instill doubt, hesitation, and uncertainty into his opponents. If the server has a variety of serves, he can keep the receiver mentally off-balance, unable to anticipate the serve and prepare an effective return.

Effective servers should have an arsenal of at least three serves. (I like to have four: a lob serve, a slice serve, topspin serve, and a low, flat serve.)   And the server should be able to hit all of his serves to either side of the service area.

But, if the server fails to take advantage of his opportunity ….. if he serves the same, easily anticipated serve time after time ….. then the opportunity passes to the service receiver.

In preparation for the opportunity provided by ineffective servers, service receivers should have at least three returns in their arsenal. (Again, I like to have four: a lob return, a short, angled return, a top spin return, and a low, flat return. The return that I select for each serve to me depends on the serve. If I can

Section III --- Physical Aspects

anticipate the type of serve, I can prepare the most effective return against it. And if the serve allows me to select from my types of returns, I will be able to vary my returns to keep the serving team at a disadvantage.

In nearly every sport where the initiating player can obtain a tactical advantage, he uses that advantage. But, in pickleball, servers very seldom develop and utilize a variety of serves. This failure is doubly discouraging because the serving team already starts at a disadvantage. (The receiving team has the first opportunity to move forward to the NVZ while the serving team has to remain back awaiting the bounce of the service return.)

A good server could reduce the receiving team's advantage by employing a variety of serves. But few servers do so. Watch servers……..even high level players. Notice that most of them seem to believe that serving is just a way to start each rally. They don't appear to think of their serves as offensive weapons.

In any given game, I may not use all four of my serves or all four of my service returns. I'll probably use at least three of each. I'll certainly use at least two of each. I'll select which serves (and service returns) to use based on the strengths and weaknesses of my opponents, the score, the type of tactical game that my partner and I want to play, and the environmental conditions.

The serves and returns that you develop may be different than my favorites. But yours should differ from each other enough that your opponent won't be able to anticipate and prepare for it. Because you want to discourage the service returner from joining his partner at the NVZ, most of your serves should be deep. An occasional short, angled serve might be warranted just to add to his confusion.

Likewise, if you are returning serve, most of your returns should be deep to discourage the serving team from moving forward.

"OK", you say, "I'll develop several serves. But how do I know when to use each one?"

You'll need to decide that for yourself. But I can give you some examples of how I decide.

Early in each game, I try to hit a variety of serves to each opponent. I observe their reactions closely to ascertain which serves give each opponent the most difficulty. For the rest of the game, I will still hit a variety of serves to each opponent just to keep him off-balance. But, I will be sure to give each of them many serves they have difficulty with.

I also observe the receiver's initial position on the court, the type of returns he hits, his general style of play, and the environmental conditions. I select serves based on those factors. Here are specific examples of how I decide which serves to use in any given situation:

LOB SERVE:
    -- When the receiver is standing on, or inside, his baseline. (I know that he'll have to step back to hit it, thereby slowing his approach to the NVZ
    -- When, outdoors, there's a cross-wind blowing. (A lobbed serve blowing sideways across the court can be very difficult to return.)
    --When my opponents are bangers. (Many bangers have difficulty banging a ball that bounces above their waist.)
    -- When the receiver is slow at getting to the NVZ. (A lobbed serve will make him even slower.)

SLICE SERVE:
    --When the receiver likes to hit his returns close to a side line. (The slice will often cause his return to drift out of bounds.)

TOPSPIN SERVE:

--When the receiver likes to hit his returns close to my baseline. (The topspin will often cause his return to carry long. This serve is particularly effective outdoors when the receiver has a wind from behind him. The wind will add to the distance of his return, making it even more likely to go long.)

LOW, FLAT SERVE:

-- When the receiver tends to hit low, hard shots into the net.
-- When the receiver moves from a normal receiving position to protect a weak backhand.
-- When the receiver has mobility problems.
-- Outdoors when I'm serving into a headwind. (The headwind will slow the ball and lower its bounce height, increasing the probability that the receiver will hit it into the net.

As you can see, not only is it important to have a variety of serves in your arsenal. It's also important to wisely select your serves to each opponent in every game.

Ron

Section III --- Physical Aspects

COURT POSITION --- MAKING HARD SHOTS LOOK EASY

When you make an amazingly difficult shot, is it because your opponent forced you to? Or is it because you weren't in the correct position on the court to make an easy shot?

If you watch great players, the one thing they have in common is that they make their shots look easy.

To play your best, constantly assess your position on the court relative to the other three players and the ball. Anticipate your opponents' shots and put yourself in the most logical position to effectively defeat the most likely shot BEFORE THEIR SHOT IS HIT.

Pickleball Pointers

Perhaps when you make a difficult shot, your partner should ask: **"How did you get so far out of position!?!?!?!?!"** rather than saying: **"Great shot!"**

Ron

Section III --- Physical Aspects

KEEP YOUR EYE ON THE BALL

Everyone understands that, to hit a pickleball, you must keep your eye on it. But I'd suggest that to play pickleball effectively, you need to watch the ball AT ALL TIMES.

As I discussed in "COURT POSITION --- MAKING HARD SHOTS LOOK EASY", you should constantly assess your position on the court relative to the other three players and the ball. You can only do that if you are watching the ball.

In addition, if a ball is hit to your partner, you are responsible for deciding whether it is IN or OUT. Your partner is busy hitting the ball.

You can better assess its location than your partner can. If your partner knows he can count on you to assess the location of the ball, he can concentrate on hitting it well.

It is particularly critical to watch the ball when your partner is returning serve and you are at the net. If you see the ball come off of your partner's paddle and know where it is going, you can anticipate the potential returns from the opposition and position

Pickleball Pointers

yourself appropriately. In addition, you have, by far, the better look at whether a short serve is in the NVZ.

Ron

Section III --- Physical Aspects

PERIPHERAL VISION

I need for you to participate in a little test with me.

Stand up. (Come on. Do it. This will be enlightening. I promise.)
Face directly forward.
Extend your dominate arm directly out to your side at shoulder height.
Continuing to look straight ahead, how well can you see your hand?

Practically not at all. Right?

Now, without turning your head, turn your eyes as far as you can toward your outstretched hand. How well can you see your hand?

Still not very clearly. Right?

What does this little test tell us about pickleball? It tells us, that unless you turn your head, you cannot clearly see your paddle contact a ball that is even with you. Actually, your area of clear vision is only about a 9 degree arc. The only way you can clearly see your paddle contact a pickleball is to look almost directly at the point of impact.

And the only way you can always look directly at the point of impact is to TURN YOUR HEAD.

Have you ever completely missed an easy overhead slam?
Do you sometimes hit routine shots with the edge of your paddle? These types of misses are practically impossible if you can clearly see the ball as your paddle impacts it.

I'm going to make two absolute statements.

    1. IN ORDER TO HIT A PICKLEBALL ACCURATELY, YOU MUST CLEARLY SEE THE PADDLE IMPACT THE BALL.

    2. IN ORDER TO CLEARLY SEE THE PADDLE IMPACT THE BALL, YOU MUST TURN YOUR HEAD.

Don't rely on peripheral vision.
Don't just swivel your eyes.
Make it a point of emphasis.
Every time you hit a ball, turn your head so that you are looking directly at the point of contact.

Section III --- Physical Aspects

If necessary, exaggerate the head turns until it becomes a habit. This is one of the techniques on which you are very likely to backslide. You will need to regularly check yourself.

Some players think they are seeing the ball hit their paddle. But they aren't. How can you tell if you are actually focusing on the ball, not just looking in its direction?
If you can see the holes in the ball all the way to your paddle,
Or
If you can see the spin on the ball all the way to your paddle,
you are certainly focusing on the ball with your direct vision.

So watch the holes or watch the spin on every shot hit at you, and you'll see your game improve.

Ron

THREE STROKES

Recently I've noticed that many players use the same type of stroke regardless of their position on the court and the tactical situation. That is like a golfer playing a round of golf with only one club. Golfers need a whole bag of clubs to play a round of golf. Pickleball is simpler. You only need three strokes to play effectively.

THREE STROKES YOU NEED TO MASTER

SWING

--Full, smooth backswing and a full, smooth stroke with long follow through.

--The most powerful of the three strokes.

--Used primarily from the baseline area.

PUNCH

--Little or no backswing, just a straight ahead stroke.

--Keep your paddle up and close to your chest to be prepared to strike with this shot.

--Much easier to execute if you let the ball get close enough to you that you can hit it with your elbow bent.

Section III --- Physical Aspects

--Used at the NVZ to react quickly and aggressively to short shots.

LIFT

--Just pick up the ball with the paddle and let it drop over the net.
--No backswing, but follow through.
--Don't think of it as a hit .... just a lift and follow through.
--It's your dinking weapon.
--Easier to implement if you hit the ball diagonally across the net rather than directly in front of you.

Watch some 5.0 players and you'll see how they use three different strokes.

If you develop and use the appropriate stroke, your game should become much more effective.

Ron

Pickleball Pointers

DOING WHAT COMES NATURALLY

Some tennis players play pickleball from the baseline.
Some racquetball players slam every pickleball shot.
Some ping pong players spin every pickleball shot.
Some new pickleball players stay back from the kitchen so they can defend themselves against slammers.

What do all of these pickleball players have in common?
They are all doing what comes naturally to them. Unfortunately a player's natural tendencies aren't necessarily the optimum way to play pickleball.

It is true that some of these players can win some games. But I would argue that they would win many more games if they would learn to play the game correctly. I would suggest that if you want to be the best pickleball player that your physical abilities will allow, learn to play the game correctly.

Follow the Four Commandments.

Section III --- Physical Aspects

Attempt to hit the correct shots, even if you miss them. That's the only way to improve. Don't hit shots just because your background makes you naturally comfortable with them.

Ron

Pickleball Pointers

___INTO THE VALLEY OF DEATH___

"'Forward the Light Brigade!'
Was there a man dismayed?
Not, though the soldier knew
Someone had blundered.
Theirs not to make reply,
Theirs not to reason why,
Theirs but to do and die.
Into the valley of Death
Rode the 600".

This is the second stanza of the famous poem by Alfred Lord Tennyson, "The Charge Of The Light Brigade." But what can this poem possibly have to do with pickleball?

The poem immortalizes the story of 600 brave men who, following orders, charged headlong into overwhelming firepower of the enemy.

I'm afraid that pickleball coaches, clinics, and videos have inadvertently caused many players to, rhetorically, charge into the valley of Pickleball Death.

Many players, through reticence or lack of understanding of pickleball tactics, fail to move forward to the Non Volley Zone. Consequently, coaches, clinics, and videos stress the absolute need to go forward. Unfortunately, many players, blindly following that guidance, hit shots that can be easily slammed by their opponents and then charge bravely, but futilely, into the slam.

As instructors, we should be teaching our students that they must learn to hit shots that can't be readily slammed, and then move to the NVZ as soon as it is safe to do so.

Let me be completely clear about this.

If you want to win, you must get SAFELY to the NVZ.

If you want to get SAFELY to the NVZ, you must learn to hit shots from your baseline that your opponents can't attack (slam).

If you hit a shot from the baseline that your opponents can slam, you must stay back at your baseline and try to return the slam with a shot that can't be slammed. When you successfully hit a shot that can't be attacked, you must take advantage of the opportunity and move to the NVZ immediately.

Ron

Section III --- Physical Aspects

<u>WINNING IS ONLY A STEP AWAY</u>

Watch a few 5.0 or Professional games on YouTube. But don't watch the ball or the players' paddles. Just pick a player and watch his feet. Watch how often his feet move. Watch how his feet put him in position to cover the court. Watch how his feet put him in position to hit a shot without reaching, or twisting, or becoming unbalanced. 5.0 players step to get in the optimum position to hit each shot.

Because 5.0 players step to get in the correct position, their upper body makes the same shot, with the same motions, time after time. So it's easy for them to hit accurate shots. This is especially obvious when they are dinking. They can hit dink after dink after dink without a miss. Compare that with the dinking of intermediate players.

Now watch local recreational players. Notice how often they lean for a shot rather than stepping to it. Notice how often they are off-balance. Notice how often they stand flat-footed at one place on the court rather than moving in response to the location of the ball, the location of their partner, and the location of their opponents.

Because intermediate players lean, their upper bodies are in a different position for each shot. Each shot is made in a unique position so it's very difficult to achieve consistent results.

Want to be a better player? Then use better footwork to put yourself in the correct position to hit good shots.

Truly, winning is only a step (or two) away.

Ron

Section III --- Physical Aspects

YOU'RE NOT TOO SLOW

I see many, many players who don't reach shots that they should, and hit shots while they are still moving when they should be able to stop first. When I mention this to them, their usual response is: "I'm just too slow." It's been my observation that they aren't really too slow. They are simply making two errors that keep them from getting to shots.

TWO PHYSICAL ERRORS THAT MAKE PLAYERS SLOW

1. They don't prepare to respond immediately to their opponents shots. They stand upright, on their heels, with their paddles down. (Merely standing upright with weight on your heels will cost you two steps.)

2. After they hit a shot, they don't immediately move to the most advantageous position in preparation for their next shot. Some players seem to simply enjoy watching their shots. Other players play a reactive game. They simply wait until their opponents hit a shot, then run toward it. (This will cost you one to four steps, depending on what type of shot you are trying to reach.)

THE SOLUTION

If you want to be "faster":

1. Prepare for EVERY shot by assuming the correct ready position.

    -- Balanced

    -- Knees bent

    -- Weight forward on balls of feet

    -- Paddle in front of chest

    -- Eyes focused intently on the ball

    -- Mentally ready to move instantly

2. After you follow through on every one of your shots you must immediately move to the most advantageous location for your next shot and assume your ready position.

Neither one of these two solutions comes naturally to most players. You'll probably need to consciously focus on these two skills in order to improve.

The effort will be well worthwhile.

Ron

Section III --- Physical Aspects

IT'S ALL NEWTON'S FAULT

Newton's First Law Of Motion states, "EVERY OBJECT IN A UNIFORM STATE OF MOTION TENDS TO REMAIN IN THAT STATE OF MOTION UNLESS AN EXTERNAL FORCE IS APPLIED TO IT."

"WOW", you say. "Ron has really gone off the deep end this time! What can this have to do with my pickleball play?"

Newton's First Law tells us that if you are moving on the court, it will require force (and consequently time and distance) for you to stop.

Think of all the times you have been moving on the court when an opponent's shot went past you. And you thought to yourself: "I should have been able to get to that ball!"

It's not your fault. It's Newton's fault!

You didn't get to the ball because Newton decreed that it takes force (thus time and distance) for you to stop. And more force to move in another direction. The ball went past you while you were trying to stop and/or change direction. If you had been stopped, your reaction time would have been greatly decreased.

Because it's a natural law, you can't ignore Newton's First Law. However, you can make sure that it doesn't apply to you. Simply stop and prepare to return your opponent's shot before he hits it.

The next time a ball whizzes past you as you are moving, just remember IT'S ALL NEWTON'S FAULT! Resolve that you won't let Newton beat you again. Resolve that you'll stop in time to be ready to return your opponent's shots.

Before your opponent hits his shot, Stop, Bend your knees to lower your center of gravity, and Lean forward to get your weight on the balls of your feet.

You'll have minimized the adverse effect of Newton's First Law on your play. And you will maximize the number of shots you can reach.

Ron

Section III --- Physical Aspects

YOU SHOULD BE IN THE MOVIES

Have you ever heard your own voice played back from a recorder? It doesn't sound at all like you thought it did, does it?

I suspect that the same thing is true of your play on the court. I suspect that your play isn't at all as you think it is. You are probably out of position without realizing it. I suspect that you often reach for shots when you should step. Etc., etc., etc.

I believe it would be very beneficial to your play if you could have yourself recorded for a few games and study those recordings.

I believe that you'd see lots of areas for improvement that you're not even aware of.

If you get an opportunity to be recorded and later study your play, I'd urge you to do so.

Ron

GAMES VERSUS DRILLS

I think it's safe to say that we all go to the pickleball courts because we really like to play the game. More than that, I think it's also true that nearly all of us really like to WIN games.

If you consider playing to be merely a social endeavor and don't really care about winning, then don't bother to read further. But if you like to win………………………

There are two ways to consistently win games. One way is to play against opponents with inferior skills/experience. The other way to win consistently is to improve your own skills.

Playing against inferior players doesn't provide much of a sense of accomplishment. If you want to win against your equals or superiors, you need to improve your skills.
Unfortunately, playing games is not a good way to improve your skills. In fact, playing games will often cause your skills to plateau, if not atrophy. The reasons for that aren't necessarily inherently obvious, so let's explore them.

Section III --- Physical Aspects

Playing games against inferior opponents will not bring out the best in your play. It's difficult to play at your very best against opponents you can easily beat. There's not enough of an adrenalin rush to make you mentally focus or physically challenge yourself.

Playing games against your equals or superior players doesn't necessarily improve your skills either. "But, why is that?" you ask. Because in tough games, you are under much pressure to hit shots that you are most comfortable with, even if they are not the technically correct shot that you need to hit to improve your skills.

In a tough game, you aren't likely to practice that third shot drop that you can only hit occasionally. You'd look like a poor teammate if you did.

On the other hand, drills allow you to practice a variety of technically correct shots without the pressure of playing a game and/or letting a partner down.

Unless you drill regularly, you will simply never hit enough of the difficult shots to become confident in them. Consequently, you won't use them in a game.

If you drill consistently, you will become confident in a much wider variety of shots. Consequently, you will have a much broader arsenal of shots at your disposal. That variety will minimize your weaknesses and allow you to become a chameleon, taking advantage of your opponents' weaknesses.

Drills are especially efficient at raising your skill level when you do them within organized classes. An organized class will force you to spend enough time on each drill to become confident in the shot(s) it's teaching. And you'll have an instructor/coach to correct your errors as you learn.

Drills aren't as much fun as playing. But drills don't have to be boring either. You can make drills fun. For example, when you're doing dinking drills, see how many times you can dink without a miss. See how many times each of you can hit your serve within six feet of the baseline without a miss, etc. etc. Keep track. Put some pressure on yourself. Play for a prize. Loser buys the winner a Coke.

I've read that doing drills will improve your skills five times faster than playing games will. In my experience, drills are far more efficient than that. I'd estimate that drills are ten to twenty times more effective than playing games.

Section III --- Physical Aspects

I highly encourage you to:

--participate in every class available to you;

--find a few other players who want to focus on improving and spend at least 15 to 30 minutes on drills every time you go to the court.

Remember the old saying, "Practice makes perfect."?
In recent years, the fallacy of that saying has become obvious.
Now we say "Perfect practice makes perfect."

If you're going to do drills, make sure that you are doing them properly. Drill with a player who is skilled enough to know how to do the drill correctly. Or drill under the supervision of a qualified coach or instructor.

Ron

SECTION IV --- MENTAL ASPECTS

<u>ELEVEN IS A SMALL NUMBER</u>

Most pickleball games are played to 11, so each point is very important. Every point that you unnecessarily lose reduces your chance of winning the game by about 9%. Every service opportunity that you waste by missing a serve also reduces your chance by 9%.

Wise players recognize that every point is crucial. They focus on each individual shot in every rally as if it were the only one because:

ELEVEN IS A SMALL NUMBER!

Ron

Pickleball Pointers

PLAYING WITH A PURPOSE

By "Playing With A Purpose", I don't mean a general purpose such as winning the game. I mean playing each shot with a purpose.

Do you play each shot with a purpose? I'm afraid that many players don't.

SERVING WITH A PURPOSE

When you serve, is it just to get the rally started? Or do you have a specific purpose for the serve? Are you trying to give your team an advantage with the serve? Are you trying to force the opposition to make a return that you can handle? As the game goes on, do you remember your opponents' returns of your service? Do you hit a variety of serves at each opponent? Do you know which of your serves each opponent returns weakly and which he returns strongly?

It is generally accepted that the serving team starts at a disadvantage. Your serve should be calculated to reduce, or eliminate, that disadvantage. You have several options to achieve that end. If you've studied your opponents, (watched them return a variety of serves), you've probably noted that some serves they

Section IV --- Mental Aspects

return strongly and other serves they return more weakly. Some players hit backhands weakly. Some players cheat to their backhand sides to cover a weakness, and leave a large gap on their forehand sides. Some players stand a step or two inside the court, leaving themselves vulnerable to a deep (and particularly a high, deep) serve. Some players can't hit a high-bouncing serve well, so lobbed serves are effective. Some players aren't fast enough to strongly return a short serve that is angled to the side of the court. Some players don't react quickly enough to a low, hard-driven serve. And most players will return more weakly if they can't anticipate the nature of the serve, so varying the serve is effective.

The key to serving with a purpose is to serve a variety of styles to each of your opponents early in the game, note each opponent's strengths and weaknesses, and then serve to their weaknesses.

RETURNING SERVE WITH A PURPOSE

When you return a serve, is it just to get to the net? Or are you trying to obtain an even greater advantage than just being at the net? Are you trying to force the opposition to make a weak return that you can easily handle to increase your advantage at the net? As the game goes on, do you remember your opponents' returns of your service return? Do you hit a variety of returns at each server? Do you know which of your returns each opponent returns weakly and which he returns strongly?

The key to returning serves with a purpose is to return a variety of styles to each of your opponents early in the game, note each opponent's strengths and weaknesses, and then return serves to their weaknesses.

It is generally accepted that the receiving team starts with an advantage. Your serve return should be calculated to maintain, or increase, that advantage. You have several options to achieve that end. If you've studied your opponents, (watched them hit a number of serves), you've probably noted that when you return the serves, some of your returns are more effective than others at maintaining your advantage. Some players hit backhands weakly. Some players cheat to their backhand sides to cover a weakness, and leave a large gap on their forehand sides. Some players stand a step or two inside the court, leaving themselves vulnerable to a deep return. Some players aren't fast enough to strongly return a short return that is angled to the side of the court. Some players don't react quickly enough to a low, hard-driven return. And most players will return more weakly if they can't anticipate the nature of the return, so varying the return is effective. (Notice that you're

Section IV --- Mental Aspects

looking for the same weaknesses in your opponents when you receive serve as you are when you are the server.)

PLAYING WITH A PURPOSE

As you hit each subsequent shot, does it have a purpose? If you can't hit a winner, do you hit a shot calculated to increase your team's advantage on the next one or two shots?

I'd suggest that EVERY shot you hit should have a purpose, including the serve and the return of serve.

Unless your mind is calculating your choices of shots and anticipated responses for every shot of every rally, you are not playing with a purpose.

Ron

<u>REACTIVE, ACTIVE, OR PROACTIVE?</u>

Beginning players are typically Reactive. They hit a ball and wait for the opponent to return the ball. Then they run to the ball and hit it again. They do little physically, or more importantly mentally, until the ball is hit back to them. They are both physically and mentally "behind the power curve".

At some point in their development, most players move from Reactive to Active. Active players will move on the court after they hit the ball. They may even mentally consider what type of shot to expect from the opponents and prepare for it. Physically and mentally they play the shot they see developing.

The truly good player is Proactive. He continuously thinks two or three shots ahead. As a minimum, he knows the shot that he wants to hit to put the opponents at a disadvantage. He knows that his shot will limit the opponents' choice of shots, and he knows what shot he will hit in response to the opponent's return of his first shot. Each time the ball is hit, the Proactive player

Section IV --- Mental Aspects

regenerates and renews his thinking to remain ahead of the play by at least two shots.

The Proactive player's goal is to CONTROL each rally ---- to force his opponents to hit shots that he has anticipated, and to know how to respond to that opponent's shot.

I suspect that many players never get mentally beyond the Active stage of development. If you are Proactive, you can beat them even if they have better physical skills than you do.

How many shots ahead do you think?

Ron

PICKLEBALL --- THE MENTAL GAME

You will play against three types of pickleball opponents – those that are physically less skilled than you, those that are about equal in physical skill to you, and those that are physically better than you.

There is no glory in beating physically inferior players. There is only glory in beating your physical equals and physical superiors. But how do you achieve such glory? Fortunately for you, you have an asset that your opponents may not be using --- your brain.

It seems to me that most players concentrate on improving their physical skills, not their mental skills. So you can tip the balance in your favor even though you may be physically outmatched.

"WOW!" you say, "How do I do that?"

Section IV --- Mental Aspects

It's very, very simple. If their best shots will beat your best shots, don't let them hit their best shots. Make them play their worst shots against your best shots.

Observe their shots early in the game. Force them to hit shots at which they are weakest. Force them to hit into your strengths. Play With A Purpose. Be Proactive. You can beat many opponents mentally that you could not beat physically.

Take as your role models, King Leonidas and his 300 Trojans at Thermopylae Pass in 480 BC. Through tactics, skill, and bravery, they held off the attack by an overwhelmingly stronger force of 100,000 Persian invaders for three days. Even though they were eventually defeated by betrayal, their exploits covered them with immortal glory.

Ron

A DICHOTOMY?

"Dichotomy (noun) ---something with seemingly contradictory qualities; a contradiction."

Here's an example of an apparent dichotomy: **In order to play your best, you cannot care whether you win or lose.**

WOW! That certainly seems like a dichotomy, doesn't it? But it's not a dichotomy. It's absolutely true.

And I don't mean just mouthing the words "I don't care if I win or lose." I mean absolutely not caring in the deepest part of your soul.

By "not caring" I don't mean that you are lackadaisical or half-hearted in your approach. I mean that you care intensely about playing your best, but not at all about the outcome of that play. I suspect that this concept will be a hard sell to many of you. But let me try.

Section IV --- Mental Aspects

The subconscious mind is very powerful, much more powerful than the conscious mind, much more powerful than most people even suspect.

If the conscious mind wants to win something badly, the subconscious mind can sense that as a fear of failure. The stress between the conscious and subconscious causes a tremendous stress on the brain. The subconscious wants to alleviate that stress as quickly as possible. And that fear of failure can cause the subconscious mind to force failure upon you.

Every coin has two sides. The conscious mind's desire to win is, in the subconscious mind, a fear of losing. And the subconscious mind is far more powerful than the conscious mind.

The subconscious fear of failure can become so intense, and the resulting physical reaction to that fear so debilitating that many athletes, including professional athletes, have been forced to quit the sport they love. They simply cannot execute even the most basic skills of the sport. Their subconscious mind will not allow it.

This subconscious fear has a thousand faces. Golfers and baseball players call it "The Yips". Archers and firearms competitors know it as "Target Panic". And hunters talk about "Buck Fever".

Regardless of the name given it, it is the same disease. It is the physical inability to execute the skills needed in a sport because fear of failure in the subconscious mind will not allow it. Just Google "The Yips", "Target Panic" and "Buck Fever", and you can read pages and pages on the topics.

So how do you avoid being your own worst enemy on the court?

I would propose to you that at a gut level, you absolutely must believe that winning does not matter. "Winning" or "Losing" are emotional thoughts. If you think about winning, each good thought will raise your hopes and each bad shot will increase your fears and self-doubts. And your emotions will contribute to your downfall. Instead, focus on playing each rally to the best of your ability.

In truth, you have very little control over whether or not you win. The skill of your opponents may well determine who wins and who loses. However, you have total control over whether you hit each shot and play each rally to the best of your ability. Your goal should be to finish the match knowing that you have played each rally as well as you could.

Section IV --- Mental Aspects

Refuse to worry about previous shots. Just calmly learn from them and move on. One day recently, I wasn't playing well. I missed a routine slam, and that discouraged me. My partner sensed my negative emotion and reminded me that: "The only shot that counts is the next one." (Great partner!!!)

Focus totally on execution of the current shot and taking control of the current rally. Any emotion (either positive or negative) can cause you to lose focus.

Memories of previous shots and rallies should have only one purpose for you ---- to study the previous shots and rallies, learn from them, and use the information to play the next rally.

I understand that this dichotomy is far easier to understand than it is to implement. But it's absolutely essential if you want to play at your highest level.

Ron

THE ZONE

Most sports enthusiasts have heard of The Zone. Many players have achieved it. It is a goal you should strive for in pickleball.

But what is The Zone? The Zone is a level of conscious/subconscious interaction that allows you to play far above your normal physical ability. It will allow you to make shots you shouldn't even be able to reach --- to return slams that are so hard your conscious mind doesn't even have time to react --- to know instinctively where/how to hit a winning shot.

The Zone can be achieved in most physical sports from rifle shooting to basketball, to ping pong, to pickleball. In the past, I have achieved it in several sports including softball and archery. So I know what it feels like. Now I know it can be achieved in pickleball because I played pickleball in The Zone for the first time today --- not in every game --- not for every shot ---- but often enough to recognize the old feeling.

Although many people know of The Zone, few people know the keys to achieving it. Let me see if I can explain how I try to achieve it. As I said above, it is a melding of the conscious and subconscious minds. Here are the keys as I feel them.

FOCUS --- To reach The Zone, I must focus intently on the game I'm playing, and particularly on the rally I'm playing. I must really be "into the game". I can't get there if I'm playing half-heartedly. I can't get there if I'm distracted by other games or background conversations around me. I can't get there if I'm playing inferior players that I can beat with my conscious mind.

ATTITUDE --- I can't reach The Zone if I'm worried about winning or losing. I must be playing each rally for the sheer love of playing. If I'm worried about winning (or about anything else for that matter), my conscious mind won't let go enough to allow my subconscious mind to take over. I can't worry about rallies previously lost or rallies in the future. I must concern myself only with the current rally.

CALMNESS --- Not only must I focus and be free of distractions, but, even more, my conscious mind must be calm and confident. My conscious mind must be willing to let go, to let my subconscious mind take over. My conscious mind must feel as if I have control of the point, that I can dictate what my opponents must do. And I can overcome them.

SLOW MOTION --- I envision the game moving in slow motion. I try to see each shot, both from me and from my opponents, as if it were in slow motion. I don't let my mind feel as if it's being rushed.

PHYSICAL SUPPORT TO THE ZONE --- In response to my conscious mind, my body stalks the court as if I were stalking prey. As with the calmness of my mind, I don't let my body rush. I move to the ball early, hit it, and move quickly, but unhurriedly to the optimum position for my next shot.

I don't know how to better describe The Zone and how to reach it. I do know that when you reach it, you will recognize the feeling. You'll know it immediately.

Sometimes a little appropriate music can help you understand a teaching point. **The greatest** song ever written about The Zone was written for the rock opera Tommy. It's called "Pinball Wizard" by the Who. Watch it on YouTube.

Section IV --- Mental Aspects

It's well worth watching. You'll probably want to turn your speakers up a little!!!!!

Ron

Pickleball Pointers

<u>NOTABLE QUOTES</u>

"Don't give up. Don't ever give up."   Coach Jimmy Valvano, basketball coach at North Carolina State

In 1993, while dying of cancer, Coach Valvano included this guidance in a memorable speech. Coach Valvano teaches us that we should not be discouraged if we are behind our opponents in the score. Just play our very best until the game is over. Coach Valvano's speech is one of the most inspirational speeches ever given. Even though it's 25 years old, it's still available on YouTube. Just look for it as "Jim Valvano's Famous "Never Give Up... Don't Ever Give Up Speech at 1993 ESPYs".

"Now remember, when things look bad and it looks like you're not gonna make it, then you gotta get mean. I mean plumb, mad-dog mean. 'Cause if you lose your head and you give up then you neither live nor win.
That's just the way it is."   Josey Wales in "The Outlaw Josey Wales"

There's no way that written words could adequately convey Josey's message. To understand, you need to watch the scene.

Fortunately, like everything else these days, that scene is easily found on YouTube. Just search for the first few words.

Yeah, I know that pickleball isn't a life or death situation (at least not for most of us). But there is a lesson to be taken from that scene.

Let me adapt the scene to pickleball.

"Now remember, when things look bad and it looks like you're not gonna win, you gotta focus on every shot of every rally. I mean totally focus. 'Cause if you lose your head and you give up then you can't win.

That's just the way it is."

"Don't strive to win. Strive to succeed." **Coach John Wooden, basketball coach for UCLA**

Coach Wooden defines winning as having the higher score. He defines succeeding as playing your hardest, giving your all on the field of competition. He notes that you have little control over who wins. But you have complete control over whether you succeed. And, he adds, if you strive too hard to win, you may actually hurt your chances of succeeding (of playing your best). This is exactly what we discussed in "A Dichotomy?" above.

Coach Wooden gave a TED speech Coach Wooden on the subject of wining versus succeeding. Search "ted.com john wooden on the difference between winning and losing".

"It ain't over 'til it's over." Yogi Berra, catcher for the New York Yankees

Yogi reminds us that being ahead in points is meaningless. Never relax just because you're ahead in points. Play every rally to the very best of your ability until the game is over.

Or, in the words of Kenny Rogers in "The Gambler": *"You never count your money when you're sittin' at the table. There'll be time enough for countin' when the dealings done."*

"The ability to gain victory by changing and adapting according to the opponent is called genius." Master Sun Tzu, Chinese military strategist over 2000 years ago. (Sun Tzu is still studied as a military genius.)

And, again, Master Sun Tzu tells us:
"Know your enemy and know yourself and you can fight a hundred battles without disaster."

Section IV --- Mental Aspects

Master Sun Tzu teaches that being able to change and adapt to your opponents, identifying and preying on their weaknesses with your strengths as the match progresses, is the key to victory.

Ron

Pickleball Pointers

MY PHILOSOPHICAL EVOLUTION

In this chapter, I'm going to bare my soul a little.

I've never been athletically gifted in any sport. To be even moderately successful, I've always had to work hard, both physically and mentally.

When I first started playing pickleball, all I wanted to do was get the ball over the net. I wasn't good, but I was having a great time trying. And I wanted to improve, so I began to study the game and play harder.

As I gained experience and expertise, my goal evolved to winning games. Winning was fun. (But losing wasn't. And if I was having an "off" day, or if I had less experienced partners, pickleball wasn't much fun at all.)

I thought about that a while.

After some mental deliberation with myself, I realized that I'm never going to be a world class pickleball player. There will always be players that I can't beat. In the first place, I've never been

Section IV --- Mental Aspects

physically gifted. In the second place, I'm 72 years old, and I have two bad shoulders and a bad knee. Who do I think I'm kidding?

So my philosophy toward pickleball evolved again. I still like to win. And I still dislike losing. (If you don't want to win, there's no reason to walk onto the court.) But, more importantly, I want to play to the best of my ability every point of every game. And I want to be the best partner I can be regardless of the skill level of my partner. And most importantly, I want every point of every game to be fun.

What's your philosophy?

Does it allow you to have fun every time you step on the court?

Ron

<u>RECREATIONAL PLAY VS. TOURNAMENT PLAY</u>

Do you play better during recreational play than you do in a tournament? If so, perhaps it's a psychological problem.

Many athletes perform better in practice than they do in formal games. (Recreational play is somewhat analogous to practice, whereas a tournament is a formal game – a formal, public test of your skills). In practice, there's less pressure to perform well. Players don't become mentally anxious. Their calm minds can let their skills play the game to their fullest physical abilities. But in a formal game the pressure to perform well manifests itself in their subconscious minds as a fear of failure. And that fear will interfere with their ability to focus and play to the best of their abilities.

With a proper mental approach (playing for the love of the game), players should play at least as good in matches as they do in practice. But with an improper mental approach (making winning a life or death situation), it is impossible for any athlete to compete at his highest level.

Section IV --- Mental Aspects

Mentally compare your tournament play with your recreational play. If your tournament play is inferior to your recreational play, perhaps you should reassess your emotional approach to your tournament play.

Ron

ZEN AND THE ART OF PICKLEBALL

I play my best when my mind is calm. Occasionally I can achieve a state of mental calmness where the game almost seems to go into slow motion. I easily hit shots that I ordinarily couldn't reach.

But, to reach that state, my conscious mind must let go. It must allow my subconscious mind to take over. The conscious mind cannot operate rapidly enough to return slams or make that initial first movement that allows me to reach impossible shots.

To reach that Zen-like state, I must first slow down my body. If my body is rushing to shots, my conscious mind won't be confident enough to let go.

So, if you'd like to try Zen And The Art Of Pickleball, just walk (don't run) confidently through a game. Sure, some part of your conscious mind has to keep track of the score and observe the flow of the game. But let your subconscious guide your play.

Ron

Section IV --- Mental Aspects

P A T I E N C E

Once in a while, when my team has the tactical advantage in a rally, I'll fail to take advantage of an opportunity to kill the ball. And later our opponents will win the rally. That always bothers me because I had an opportunity to win the rally, but didn't.

HOWEVER, far more often, I try to win a rally by hitting a difficult shot and I miss the shot.

For me (and I suspect for all of us) more patience, rather than less, will win more rallies. To improve my patience, I try not to think of "hitting a winner". Rather I try to think of placing each consecutive shot to gain a tactical advantage over the opponents and then increasing that advantage until my team wins the rally.

Just as an exercise, try to play a whole game without ever trying to hit a winner. Focus on just hitting good, safe shots that put your opponents in a worse and worse position until they give you the point. I think you'll find the results interesting.

Ron

GOOD DAYS AND BAD DAYS

Life is just a long series of good days and bad days strung together.

Then you die.

There is absolutely no way to escape the day-to-day variations in our lives that cause us to call one day "good" and one day "bad". Inasmuch as this is an axiomatic truth for every aspect of our lives, it is certainly true for our days on the pickleball courts. There is simply no escaping bad days on the court. But there are both physical and mental steps we can take to mitigate the effects of bad days.

PHYSICAL MITIGATION

Some days our coordination is below par. Some days we are tired or sore or have outside negative emotions that affect our physical abilities. You know those days .... the days when the close shots just miss, the days when you feel half a step behind.

When you see that sort of day unfolding, change your physical approach to the game. Instead of attempting to hit those tough shots next to the boundaries, stick with more conservative shots. Give yourself more leeway for error. Don't allow yourself to rush. Force yourself to slow down. Make a good approach, hit, and follow through for each shot.

MENTAL MITIGATION

When you're having a bad day on the court, it's easy to expand the importance of pickleball far beyond its actual importance to your life. It's important that you keep pickleball in a reasonable philosophical perspective.

Scientists now believe that in a few billion years, our sun will start to run out of fuel. The sun will then expand, incinerating all of the inner planets including Earth. Let's stop and think about that in depth for a moment. No more life of any kind on this planet. No more Earth. No more solar system.

I know that catastrophe won't affect me personally, but it's still very difficult for me to emotionally accept.

In comparison to the fate of our planet, missing a shot in a pickleball game really isn't that important, is it?

Pickleball Pointers

In fact, pickleball probably isn't even the most important part of each of our personal lives. I'd suggest that if pickleball is really all you live for, perhaps you should reevaluate your life.

There, that should put a bad day of pickleball back into its proper place in your priorities!

Ron

Section IV --- Mental Aspects

WHEN YOU'RE HAVING A BAD DAY

We all have bad days on the court. Days when our game is a little out of sorts. Days when we miss shots we would ordinarily make. And it seems like the harder we try, the worse our game gets.

Frustrating, isn't it?

So, how do we get out of the playing death spiral?
There are two keys.

First, get past the emotional part of the problem. Remind yourself that everyone has bad days. Calm yourself.

Second, go back to the basics.

Get into position early so you can be stopped and ready when you hit shots.

Focus on watching your paddle hit the ball on every shot.

Pickleball Pointers

Hit safer, high percentage shots down the middle. Avoid low percentage angle and outside line shots.

Take pace off the ball. Slow the game down.

If you do these things, you should be able to minimize the effects of those bad days.

Ron

BACKSLIDING

All of us naturally tend to backslide. It's simply human nature. This is true in our pickleball play as well as in many other areas of our lives.

If you find the quality of your play stagnating, or even worse regressing, you need to go back and examine all of the basic building blocks of your skills. I'll bet that you find one, or more, basic skills that you aren't executing as well as you should.

Review your play against each of the Four Commandments and their Corollaries.
If necessary, review all of this book as well as YouTube training videos.

Have a coach, mentor, or skilled player observe and critique your play.

Once you have identified the specific areas of your game that have regressed, you'll need to focus intently on executing those skills correctly until correct execution becomes automatic.

Pickleball Pointers

Being human, you can't avoid occasionally backsliding. But if you recognize the problem quickly, analyze it, and rectify it, your game should continue to improve.

Ron

Section IV --- Mental Aspects

SEVERAL GREAT SHOTS AND

.... A MISS!

Did you ever notice how often your partner makes a series of consecutive great saves and shots during a rally? (Your opponents seem to be picking on him, but he's holding his own.) Then when the ball finally comes to you, you miss a relatively easy shot.

My observation has been that it happens to all of us far more often than mere chance would indicate. After studying on the phenomenon for a while, I think I've isolated the cause.

If the ball is hit to my partner multiple times in a row during one rally (and particularly if my partner makes especially good shots), I mentally become a fascinated observer of the action, rather than a participant. And, some part of my mind really expects the rally to be over before the ball is hit to me. Consequently, when the ball is finally hit to me, I'm not mentally prepared to hit a good shot. I've learned that, in those situations, I have to consciously force myself to be mentally prepared.

There are a couple of physical tricks that I use to help myself.

>--First, I keep my feet moving, constantly changing my position in relation to the action. As long as I keep moving to the optimum position to respond to a shot that might be hit to me, my mind stays in the game.
>
>--Second, I keep communicating with my partner. I noticed one lady professional player who says "Yours" to her partner for every ball hit to the partner. I often wondered why she did that. I now believe it was to keep herself from becoming a mental spectator.

If you notice that you sometimes become a mental spectator, try these two tricks. I think they will help.

Ron

Section IV --- Mental Aspects

SPECTATING

Pickleball is an exciting spectator sport. (Lots more exciting than watching golf, or bowling, or even tennis.) It's such an exciting spectator sport that some players even spectate when they are on the court. If you observe them closely, you'll see that when they aren't hitting the ball, they are simply standing around watching the ongoing play.

Let me be completely clear about spectating.
IF YOU ARE ON THE COURT, THERE IS NEVER A TIME WHEN YOU SHOULD BE JUST SPECTATING.

You can, and should, always be doing something to help your team win.

WHENEVER THERE IS A RALLY IN PROGRESS, YOU SHOULD ALWAYS BE DOING AT LEAST ONE OF THE FOLLOWING:
    -- Mentally assessing your alternative choices for your next shot,
    -- Assuming the correct stance in preparation for hitting a shot,
    -- Hitting a shot,

-- Moving to the most tactically advantageous position for your next shot,

-- Constantly adjusting your position based on the location of the ball and the locations of the other three players,

-- Communicating with your partner,

-- Watching balls hit toward your partner to assess whether they are In or Out,

-- When balls are hit to your partner, watching your opponents feet to make sure they aren't encroaching on the kitchen.

BETWEEN RALLIES, YOU SHOULD BE DOING THE FOLLOWING:

-- Mentally checking the score to assure that it is correct,

-- Mentally checking the location and correctness of both the server and receiver,

-- Mentally assessing the strengths and weaknesses of each opponent and conceiving strategies to avoid your opponents strengths and attack his weaknesses,

-- Communicating your assessments to your partner and coordinating your team strategy with him,

-- Adjusting your position on the court in preparation for implementing your team strategy.

Section IV --- Mental Aspects

If you are really doing all the things I've listed above you won't have any time to spectate.

If you are spectating, you probably aren't executing all of the responsibilities I've listed above.

Ron

FEET FETISH

If you want to improve your game, I'd suggest you cultivate an intense "feet fetish". (No, not "foot fetish"! That's different!)

By "feet fetish", I mean concentrating on hitting as many shots as possible at your opponents' feet.

I've had new players tell me that the game is very complicated. They don't know when to hit a drop shot, which opponent to hit at, etc. etc.

Let's simplify the game down to one basic rule of thumb:

"Hit every shot possible at your opponents' feet."

You don't have to think about when to dink, when to smash, etc. Just hit every shot at their feet and you'll automatically hit the correct type of shot.

If your opponents are at the baseline, it should be easy to hit at their feet. You can hit the ball either hard or soft at their feet. If they are both at the NVZ, you'll automatically need to dink to hit at their feet. See, focusing on hitting at their feet will automatically tell you what type of shot you need to hit.

Which of your opponents should you hit at?

Obviously, you should hit at the opponent whose feet make the easiest target.

If both of your opponents are back, hit at the weakest opponent. If one of your opponents is back and the other is at the NVZ, the feet of the opponent who is at the baseline will be the easier target. If both of your opponents are at the NVZ, hit at the weaker opponent.

Learning to hit at your opponents' feet will lead you into many other good habits. For example, in order to make it easier to hit at your opponents' feet, you'll need to move to the NVZ. That will expose their feet over the net if they are back. And it will make dinking at their feet easier if they are at the NVZ.

"But", you ask, "Aren't there times when I can hit shots that are not at my opponents' feet?" Sure there are. But you probably already do that. In fact, you probably do that FAR too often.

Pickleball Pointers

Develop a "feet fetish" and your game should improve dramatically!!!

Ron

Section IV --- Mental Aspects

IMPORTANT RALLIES

Are some rallies more important than others?

Technically, the answer is NO. Each rally is equally valuable. Each one is worth either one point or one service change.

But, psychologically, the answer may be YES.
If your opponents are susceptible to negative emotions, then the answer is definitely YES. Here are some examples of rallies that are important to putting your opponents in a negative frame of mind.

--Winning the first few rallies of a game can set a negative emotional tone for your opponents' whole game.

--Winning the first few rallies after a time out (especially if your opponent has called the time out because he is behind) can continue your opponents' downward emotional spiral.

--Winning a rally in which your opponents hit one or more really good shots can frustrate them, giving them the impression that regardless of the quality of their play, they can't win.

Pickleball Pointers

Of course, you and your partner don't suffer from these negative emotions because you know that each rally is equally valuable. Each rally is worth exactly one point or one service change.

Ron

SECTION V --- TEAMWORK

TEAMWORK

Recreational play is fun, but it isn't doubles play. Rather it's just four people on the court playing singles. It's like a "pickup" game of basketball or football. The difference between the play in a "pickup" game and the play of a team is enormous.

Recreational play is fun. But if you want the satisfaction of playing pickleball as a TEAM sport, you'll need to find one partner with whom to practice and play tournaments.

Ron

THE GOSPEL OF TEAMWORK

If you and your partner want to play as a coordinated team rather than as two players who happen to be on the same side of the net, you'll need to implement the following eight points:

1. Move up/back and left/right as a team.

2. Both members of serving team should stay BEHIND the baseline until they've made the third shot. Then they move forward or stay back as the third shot dictates. If the third shot is one that the receiving team can slam, the serving team should stay behind the baseline and play defensively until they've hit a subsequent shot that can't be slammed.

3. The serving team should not move forward until they've hit a shot that the receiving team can't drive.

4. The service receiver should hit a service return that allows him to move forward to the NVZ immediately.

5. If service receiver does not move to NVZ on his return of service, the serving team should hit a deep shot at him and then move as a unit to the NVZ.

6. There is no such thing as "my half and your half of the court". The whole court belongs to both of you.
   A. Poaching is not only allowed, it is necessary. If your partner comes to your side of the court to poach, you need to cross over to his side to cover there.
   B. If the opposition lobs over your partner, you should return the lob and your partner should switch to cover your side of the court.
   C. If your partner gets drawn outside the court by an angled shot, you need to slide to the middle of the court.

7. Have fun and encourage your partner at all times.

Ron

Section V --- Teamwork

THE GOSPEL OF COMMUNICATION

Here are the most critical keys to good communication in six easy-to-remember points.

1. Communication between teammates is vital. Communicate on every shot.
2. MINE, YOURS, SWITCH, and OUT, are the absolute minimum key words.
3. Anytime both of you go for a ball, you have failed to communicate.
4. Anytime neither of you go for a ball, you have failed to communicate.
5. If your partner is receiving the serve, watch it bounce for him to determine whether it's in or out. Call those that are out.
6. It's difficult to hit a ball and simultaneously decide whether it's in or out, so call balls Out for your partner.

Ron

BASIC AND ADVANCED COMMUNICATIONS

Several times previously, I've mentioned the importance of communications between partners. I still receive questions on the subject, so I'll try herein to be more specific.

Communication between partners is vitally important regardless of whether the two partners have played together seldom or often. If your partner does not communicate clearly, adequately, or frequently enough, you must communicate even more to compensate for your partner's inadequacies. The more often you communicate, the more automatic, natural, and effective it will become. Communicating will also keep you mentally focused on the game which will help your play.

If, due to shyness or lack of self-confidence, you choose not to communicate adequately, you and your partner cannot possibly play as a team. You'll only be two players playing singles on the same side of the net. You will have ignored a very valuable weapon.

Section V --- Teamwork

All of your communications to your partner must be stated clearly and with conviction.

BASIC COMMUNICATION RESPONSIBILITIES

Here are the absolute minimum communications for which you are responsible.

Note: The actual words that you and your partner use aren't critically important as long as you both understand the words you use.

OUT or **NO** --- A shot is hit toward your partner which you believe WILL go out. It is your responsibility to say OUT or NO to discourage him from volleying it before it goes out.

OUT --- A ball hit toward your partner lands out of bounds (including a serve to him). After it lands, it is your responsibility to call it OUT.

IN or **GOOD** --- A ball is hit toward your partner which lands in bounds and which he fails to return. It is your responsibility to call it IN or GOOD.

Pickleball Pointers

YOURS --- A shot is hit between you and your partner, or a lob is hit over you and your partner, that you want him to hit. It is your responsibility to say YOURS.

MINE --- A shot is hit between you and your partner, or a lob is hit over you and your partner, that you want to hit. It is your responsibility to say MINE.

SWITCH --- Your partner goes back to return a lob. It is your responsibility to determine whether the two of you should switch sides, and, if so, to say SWITCH.

ADVANCED COMMUNICATION RESPONSIBILITIES
Here are additional communications that you need to develop to be a great teammate.

BOUNCE IT --- A lob is hit toward your partner which you believe MAY go out. It is your responsibility to say BOUNCE IT to encourage your partner to let the ball bounce before he hits it. That way he won't volley a ball which otherwise would have gone out.

BOUNCE IT --- A short lob is hit in front of your partner. You believe that it will land short in the kitchen and bounce higher

Section V --- Teamwork

than the net. It is your responsibility to say BOUNCE IT to encourage your partner to patiently let it bounce it before hitting it strongly rather than leaning over the kitchen and hitting a weak volley.

UP or **HURRY** --- A ball is hit that will land far in front of your partner. It is your responsibility to say UP or HURRY to help him recognize that he must move forward quickly to reach the ball.

UP --- You and your partner are back near your baseline. You hit a shot that you believe you opponents cannot attack. It is your responsibility to say UP to let your partner know that you should both move to the kitchen.

BACK--- You hit a poor shot that you believe your opponents will smash. It is your responsibility to warn your partner to move rearward by saying BACK.

KILL IT or **NOW** --- A ball is hit to your partner that you believe he can put away for a winner. It is your responsibility to say KILL IT or NOW to encourage him to win the rally with his shot. Note that KILL IT doesn't necessarily mean to slam it. KILL IT merely means to win the rally. The optimum winning shot might be a smash or a dink or an angled shot or a lob. Shot choice is up to your partner.

Players have all of the above opportunities to improve their play and their teamwork through communication. Yet most players are nearly mute on the court.

Don't be like them. Be a good teammate. Practice effective communications every time you are on the court.

Ron

Section V --- Teamwork

I WANNA BOP WITH YOU, BABY

I am fortunate enough to receive the Tennis Channel. I prefer doubles tennis, so I often watch when doubles are being played. Some doubles teams are comprised of two players who specialize in doubles and play together as permanent partners. Other doubles teams are comprised of two great singles players who decide they'll play doubles together in addition to playing singles.

Often I will see a doubles match where a good doubles team is pitted against two great singles players. It's very easy to tell which team is the doubles team. They play together --- as one, whereas the two singles players often seem to be playing separate games of singles. Even though each of the singles players could beat each player of the doubles team if they were playing singles, the doubles team easily defeats the two singles players in a doubles match.

I believe there's a lesson here for us pickleball players.

When I watch local pickleball matches, it often seems as though I'm watching four singles players on the court. Seldom do I see two players on the same side of the net playing as a doubles team. Granted, it's difficult to develop team play when, playing recreationally, you have a new partner every game. It's difficult, but it's not impossible. When playing recreationally, you'll just have to put more effort into communicating and into watching your partner so you know what to expect of him.

Perhaps it would help you to play as a team if you envision a couple dancing.

Dancing with your partner on a pickleball court is not the choreographed routine that you see on "Dancing With The Stars" or in a dance competition. Rather it is an extemporaneous dance that responds to the movement and shots of your teammate and those of the opponents.

It is a dance where your goal is to communicate verbally and by observation of your partner until you automatically think, move, respond, and flow as one throughout every rally.

It is a dance where you respond appropriately to your partner's every move and every shot, and he responds appropriately to yours.

It is a dance where you understand your partner's strengths and weaknesses and he understands yours so that you are able to compensate for your partner's weaknesses with your strengths and likewise he compensates for your weaknesses with his strengths.

It is a dance where every shot you or your partner take has a purpose and that purpose is instinctually understood by both of you.

It's a dance where you and your partner both force your opponents to play their individual weaknesses against your combined strengths.

It is a dance where it is not your goal to personally hit a winning shot. Rather your goal is to weaken your opponents' positions until either you or your partner can hit a winning shot. There is no personal glory in hitting any winning shot. There is only glory in the combined effort of the team in winning the point.

It is a dance where you and your partner's minds and bodies flow together, ever pressing toward the common goal of winning the rally.

It is a dance where you see without looking, know without thinking, sense without delaying how to support your partner in every shot of each rally.

It is a dance where both you and your partner constantly and automatically adapt as one to the ebb and flow of each rally.

To test your dancing abilities, ask yourself these questions:

>---"How often do I hit a shot whose purpose is to put my partner in a position to hit a winner?"

>---"How often do I switch sides with my partner when an opponent's shot requires it?"

>---"How often do I move to cover the whole court when my partner is drawn off the court by an opponent's shot?"

>---"How often and how effectively do I communicate with my partner during a rally?"

>---"Do I think of my partner and myself as "us" or do I think of my partner as another player on the court?"

Section V --- Teamwork

---"How often do I thank my partner for hitting a shot that sets me up to hit a winner?"

---"How often do I compliment my partner for saving difficult shots, keeping us in a rally until we could take control of the rally and win it?"

Remember, in a team sport such as pickleball, it's your responsibility to be the best dance partner that you can possibly be, regardless of the dancing skill of your teammate. And it's your responsibility to do everything you can to help your teammate dance well too.

As I read over what I've written here, I realize that this is a difficult concept for me to explain. You may have to experience it yourself with a partner to understand. But, once you experience the feeling of dancing with a partner, you'll never want to play singles on a doubles court again.

Oh, yeah, you probably wonder how I selected the title to this discussion.

Pickleball Pointers

Well, it's the title of my favorite Dan Seals song, a song that always makes me smile. Just in case you need a smile too, it's on YouTube as:

"I Wanna Bop With You, Baby" Dan Seals

Ron

Section V --- Teamwork

IF YOU AIN'T RUBBIN'..................

I actually had a woman partner say to me once (in a recreational game): "You hit that ball on my side of the center line. That was my shot. Stay on your own half of the court."

I was so shocked that I didn't know how to respond. I just made certain that, for the rest of the game, I didn't reach for any shots that might land on her half of the court. Of course we lost that game. I also made certain that she and I didn't ever play on the same side of the net again.

I try to remember to tell my partner before every game: "The whole court on this side of the net belongs to both of us. Take any shot that you think you can hit more effectively than I can. Poach anytime you can."

That conversation is particularly important in recreational play where you have a new partner for each game. And it's even more important if your partner seems shy or uncertain of his ability. You need to encourage him to be aggressive.

Pickleball is a TEAM sport. To play it well, both you and your partner must play it aggressively, without regard to "my shot" or "your shot". Every shot is simply "our shot" which one of the two of you hits. The centerline on the court is merely a way to divide the service areas. It is not a line of demarcation between partners.

CAUTION: I would offer one caution. Unless you are forced to switch sides during a rally, your primary responsibility is to defend the half of the court where you started the rally. If you step in front of your partner to poach, you'd better hit a shot that doesn't allow your opponents to return the shot into the, now open, half of the court you just vacated.

NASCAR drivers have a saying: **"If you ain't rubbin', you ain't racin'!"**
In other words, if you want to win, you have to be aggressive.

Likewise, I'd suggest that, in pickleball: **"If you ain't poachin', you ain't playin'!"** As in NASCAR, if you and your partner want to win, you both have to be aggressive.

Ron

SECTION VI --- TACTICS

Pickleball Pointers

THE GOSPEL OF TACTICS

I consider the following fourteen points to be the gospel of tactics. If you implement these points consistently into your game, your tactics will never let you down.

1. Patience is your most important virtue. Don't try to force a winning shot. Play for placement until an easy winning shot is offered to you.

2. Shot placement is more important that shot speed. Never hit a shot at more than 75% of maximum power.

3. Determine your goal for each game. Is it to win that game or to improve as a player? If you want to win that game, hit the shots you are best at. If you want to improve your skills, hit shots that you need to learn (even if you miss them).

4. It's not a game of continuous movement. You should play each shot as four distinctly separate actions. They are:

Section VI --- Tactics

- A. Move – Get as close to the optimum position on the court as you can before the opponent hits his shot.
- B. Stop – Be stopped and get into ready position to hit your next shot before the opponent hits his shot.

    (It's much easier to hit a good shot from a stationary position than to hit while you're moving. Never hit a shot while you're moving unless you're forced to.)
- C. Hit The Shot – Hit the shot with good form and good follow through.
- D. Repeat A, B, and C above for the next shot.

5. Get clear to the NVZ as quickly as safely possible. Don't stop between the baseline and the NVZ unless it's absolutely necessary to be in the ready position to return a shot. Then make a return that will allow you to move forward to the NVZ.

6. Ready position is: knees bent, on balls of feet, with paddle 6" – 12" in front of your chest.

7. Position yourself on the court so that you can hit lots of forehands.

8. Doing drills will improve your game 5 to 10 times faster than just playing games.

9. "Down the middle solves the riddle." Only occasionally go for the outside.

The vast majority of your shots should be aimed at an opponent's feet or down the middle between the opponents. Those are much higher percentage shots than shots at outside lines.

10. When in trouble, dink into the NVZ.

11. Know whether each opponent is left handed or right handed. A good shot is low to opponent's backhand.

12. If a ball is below your waist, dink your return. If it's above your waist, you may dink or slam.

13. If you're at the NVZ and get driven backwards (e.g. by a lob), don't stay back. Get forward to the NVZ again ASAP.

Section VI --- Tactics

14. "At the NVZ" means toes next to the NVZ line, not a foot or two back from the NVZ.

Ron

CONTROL FREAK!!!

Being called a "control freak" is typically considered to be derogatory. Most of us try to avoid being control freaks, or at least being thought of as control freaks by our friends and family. But on the pickleball court, being a control freak is absolutely essential.

What do I mean by being a control freak on the court?
 -- I mean that I want my partner and me to control every rally.
 -- I want my partner and me to take the offensive.
 -- I want to put our opponents on the defensive.
 -- I want to bend our opponents to our will.
 -- I want to force them to hit shots weakly into our strengths.
 -- I want to force them to hit shots upward so that we can hit shots downward.
 -- I want to force them to hit shots while they are moving while we hit shots from strong stationary positions.
 -- I want to separate them, preventing them from moving as a team while my partner and I play as one.
 -- I want to create doubt and confusion in them.

But", you ask, "How is it possible to become a control freak?"

Section VI --- Tactics

The essential key is for you and your partner to be proactive. It is impossible to control rallies if you passively await your opponents' shots and then respond to them.

Each shot that you and your partner hit must have a purpose. Each shot must be calculated to improve your tactical advantage over your opponents. You must always be planning at least one shot ahead. Your mind should be saying "If I hit this shot, it will force my opponent to hit that shot. Then I'll be able to put my opponents in a worse tactical position by hitting my next shot there."

If you find your team at a tactical disadvantage, you must proactively select shots which will eliminate and then reverse the tactical situation.

Watch most players and you'll see that they are usually reactive. If you are a proactive control freak, you will be able to dictate the tactical situation, and ultimately defeat them.

Ron

Pickleball Pointers

NEVER FIGHT FAIR

Americans, in particular, seem to have a very highly developed sense of fair play. During movie fight scenes, the good guy never holds the superior weapon or superior position. It is always the bad guy who picks up the gun, knife, or club, or takes a superior position. The good guy responds with an inferior weapon, but always manages to win the fight, even from an inferior position.

While such nobility is laudable, the reality is that in pickleball, we should never fight fair. We should never give our opponents an even break – a 50% chance to win. A high noon shootout on Main Street in Deadwood between two steely-eyed gunmen isn't what we want.

Certainly we should play within both the letter and the spirit of the rules. But we should make every effort to put the opposition at a tactical disadvantage.

    --Make the opposition hit difficult shots.

    --Force the opposition into disadvantageous positions on the court.

    --Focus your shots on the weaker player and/or the player in the weaker position.

Section VI --- Tactics

--Use a variety of shots to keep your opponent off balance and uncertain in his game.

Always play within the rules. Never fight fair.

Ron

BEATING OPPONENTS WHO ARE BETTER THAN YOU

Let's start by admitting that there are players you can't beat and games you can't win.

But I believe that you should be able to win the vast majority of games against opponents who have skills equal to yours. And you should be able to win many games against opponents who are better than you.

Let's define players better than you as players whose best shots are better than your best shots.

So how do you beat players whose shots are equal to or better than yours?

It's simple. Just put them in tactical situations where they must play their worst shots against your best shots...........their weaknesses against your strengths.

Section VI --- Tactics

Early in the game, study your opponents' styles, tendencies, strengths, and weaknesses. By mid-game, you should have a very good idea of what shots you need to hit in order to force your opponents to respond with their weakest shots.

--If they like to hit from their baseline, force them into a dinking game.

--If they want to dink, hit deep shots to keep them back. If they get to the NVZ, hit offensive lobs over them.

--If they like to slam, hit deep, high lobs. Many slammers can't slam high, deep lobs.

Find ways to force them to play outside of their comfort zone, to play a game where they have few opportunities to hit shots they like to hit.

Unless your opponents' worst shots are better than your best shots, this strategy should give you a good chance of beating them.

Ron

BEATING THE BANGERS

It seems like everywhere you play, you run into a few of them..........the bangers..........those ex-tennis or ex-racquetball players who stand at the baseline smashing every pickleball they can reach. They aren't fun to play with or against. But if you can't avoid playing against them, you might as well beat them. Perhaps if you beat them often enough, they might change their ways.

WHAT DOESN'T WORK

    1. Staying back from the kitchen.

Some players, especially new players, are intimidated by bangers. These intimidated players stay back so they have more time to respond to bangs and so they won't get hurt by bangers shots. That philosophy has two problems. First, it gives bangers more of your body to slam at. Second, it encourages bangers to come to the kitchen where they can bang even more effectively.

    2. Participating in banging contests with them.

That's just playing into their strength. You need to play your strengths against their weaknesses.

    3. Hitting high, short shots that are easily attacked.

WHAT WORKS

1. Get to the kitchen.

Force the bangers into dinking contests. Most bangers don't like dinking and, consequently, aren't good at it.

2. Avoid hitting their bangs that will go out.

Bangers don't give you much time to react. So it's natural to try to return everything they hit. But doing that only encourages them to hit harder and higher bangs. If you let their wayward bangs go out, you'll win points and discourage them from continuing to bang.

3. Get to the kitchen and punch their slams back at their feet.

It's difficult to slam a shot at your feet. Note that if your punches land well in front of them, your ball may bounce high enough to be slammed, so keep your shots at their feet.

4. Hit deep, high shots.

This will have two advantages. First, it will keep the bangers back as far as possible. Second, many bangers have difficulty slamming a ball that bounces high. They are used to hitting low fast balls.

5. Hit low, short shots that aren't attackable............dinks and third shot drops.

Bangers look impressive. But, most of them have only one-dimensional games. If you force them out of their comfort zones, they aren't that hard to beat.

Remember, always play your best shots and force your opponents to hit their poorest shots.

Ron

Section VI --- Tactics

ONLY FOOLS RUSH IN

Beginning players are taught to immediately rush to the Non Volley Zone after returning a serve (or after hitting the third shot if they are the serving team). This is undoubtedly good guidance for beginners who play tentatively and need encouragement to move to the NVZ. But as players become more skilled (and play against more skilled opponents), the folly of rushing the NVZ, regardless of the tactical situation, becomes obvious.

A much better approach for intermediate and advanced players would be to rush the net AS SOON AS THE TACTICAL SITUATION ALLOWS THEM TO SAFELY DO SO.

Far too often I see intermediate players hit a short, high, easily-slammable shot and then rush blindly forward into oblivion. I'd suggest that you and your partner both rush the net only as soon as you've hit a shot that can't be slammed or hit hard and low at either of you.

(Remember, you two should ALWAYS move as a team --- forward, backward, and sideways, as the tactical situation dictates.) So, if you hit the shot, it's your responsibility to communicate the quality of your shot to your partner. If you hit the ball, it's your responsibility to say UP or BACK depending on the quality of the hit.

Ron

Section VI --- Tactics

CHAMELEONS

Do you find that you often lose games after having an initial lead (sometimes a big lead)?

Or do you find that you often come from behind (sometimes far behind) to win games?

I have a theory regarding why that happens. I think Chameleons come from behind and players who aren't Chameleons lose leads.

In the animal kingdom, chameleons constantly change their appearance to adapt to their environment. Good pickleball players do that too. They constantly change their style of play throughout the game looking for tactical advantages that will allow them to come from behind or increase their lead. And players who don't adapt and change (aren't Chameleons) are very likely to lose their initial lead in games.

Chameleon players watch their opponents closely. During the early parts of a game, opponents will reveal their strengths and their weaknesses. Chameleons note these strengths and weaknesses. During the latter parts of the game, Chameleons will force their opponents to hit their weakest shots. At the same time Chameleons will attempt to force their opponents to hit shots that will allow the Chameleons to hit their best shots.

And, the more often Chameleons play the same opponents, the earlier in the game Chameleons can take advantage of their opponents' weaknesses. So, if you're not a Chameleon, life is only going to get worse for you as you play Chameleons time after time.

My Chameleon goal is simple. I'm going to force you to hit your worst shots against my best shots all day long! It doesn't matter whether your best shots are better than my best shots if you don't get opportunities to hit your best shots.

In order for a Chameleon to be most effective, he must have a well-rounded game with minimal weaknesses. If his game is well rounded, with few weaknesses, he will be able to adapt his style of play to take best advantage of his opponents' weaknesses.
--Do you like to slam? Then, against a Chameleon, you're going to get dinked all day long.
--Do you have limited mobility or like to slam from the service line? Then, against a Chameleon, you're going to see short, angled shots all day long.

Section VI --- Tactics

--Do you hate to return lobs because lobs are sissy play? Guess what you're going to see all day long???????????

--Do you have a weak backhand? A Chameleon will pick on it incessantly.

--Do you cheat sideways on the court to cover a weak backhand? A Chameleon will see that as an invitation to hit wide to your forehand.

To be a good Chameleon, you don't have to be a perfect player. But, you should try to avoid having any serious weaknesses. A Chameleon opponent will pick on them. And those weaknesses will keep you from attacking your opponents' weaknesses most effectively.

And to be a good Chameleon Team, you and your partner must communicate what you see about your opponents and how you should attack them. You must regularly communicate between points.

As you play recreationally, watch the scores to see whether you typically lose leads or come from behind. That will be a good indication of whether you have Chameleon qualities.

Ron

LOCATION, LOCATION, LOCATION

In the real estate business, it is said that the three most important factors in determining the value of any property are: Location, Location, and Location. The same is true in pickleball. The three most important factors in determining the value of any shot are: Location, Location, and Location. The location (spot) that you hit the ball to is much more important than the speed at which you hit it.

There are two aspects of hitting a ball to the proper location: physical and mental. Competence in both is crucial, so let's talk about them both.

PHYSICAL ASPECT

Beginning pickleballers typically just try to hit the ball so it lands somewhere on the court. As we advance in skill, we try to hit the ball more accurately. But, it seems to me that somewhere about the 3.0 skill level, many of us stop improving our accuracy. It seems that when we become accurate enough to hit our serves and service returns, missing only a few of each, we think our accuracy is good enough. Then we just quit concentrating on improving our accuracy. We turn our attention to building other skills. This is certainly a mistake. We need to continue to improve the accuracy of each of our shots. Our goal should be to physically hit each shot so accurately that it lands exactly where we mentally plan for it to land.

MENTAL ASPECT

Skill at the physical aspect allows us to hit the ball to where we intend (accuracy). But that physical skill does us little good if we mentally select the wrong target.

It's been my observation that the mental aspect is usually the limiting factor in most players' ability.

Selecting the optimum target for each shot (particularly in the heat of an intense rally) is really the essence of good pickleball. It requires very rapid (sometimes almost instantaneous) calculation of a number of factors including:

--the location and direction of movement of the ball you want to hit;

--the location and direction of movement of each of your opponents;

--the location and direction of movement of your partner;

--the strengths and weakness of each of your opponents;

--the skill (accuracy) with which you can execute each of the shots in your arsenal;

--environmental conditions which might make your shot easier or harder to return.

Taken together, these factors can combine in an infinite number of ways. So there's absolutely no way for me to tell you which shot to select each time you hit the ball. But, I can tell you two things:

--You must open both your conscious and subconscious to be aware of all of the factors. You must be mentally in the flow of the game. You must teach yourself to "see" all of these factors in the few tenths of a second before you hit the ball.

-- Every shot you select should be with the intention of improving your team's tactical position on the court.

Ron

Section VI --- Tactics

AT 'EM OR AROUND 'EM

If, during a game, I were to ask each player where he directed his last shot, I think most of them would say "At the right hand opponent." or "At the left hand opponent."

Most players' tendency to hit AT an opponent is so strong that they will hit the ball at an opponent even when the other side of the court is wide open. Every time I see that happen, I always wonder what the hitter could possibly be thinking. It should be inherently obvious that hitting your shots AROUND your opponents will generally be more effective than hitting AT opponents. But if that is true, why are so many shots hit at opponents?

I believe that the answer is psychological.
Whenever we are near other people, we tend to look at them.
Whenever we communicate with other people, we look at them.

We tend to think of our opponents as "things" to be beaten.

All in all, our mental focus tends to be ON our opponents. And our shots go where we are mentally focused.

To improve the effectiveness of our shots, we need to focus on the openings between and outside of our opponents as THINGS --- as targets.

If you wanted to run safely through a forest, you would focus on the gaps between the trees, not on the trees. So it certainly is possible to focus on gaps or openings. Start thinking of your opponents as objects to be avoided. Start thinking of the gaps between and outside of your opponents as your targets.

Hit shots intended to move your opponents so that one of those gaps is increased. That will make it easier for you to hit your next shot into that gap.

The closer your opponents are to you, the more you naturally tend to focus on them. This is particularly true when all four of you are dinking at the kitchen. Far too often, I see players mindlessly dinking back and forth at each other until one of them misses.

To avoid that, I'd suggest you remember the 1960's Playtex commercial --- LIFT AND SEPARATE! To get your dinks safely over the net and drop them close to the net, concentrate on LIFTING

Section VI --- Tactics

the ball over the net rather than hitting the ball. Rather than lifting your dinks at an opponent, lift them outside one of your opponents so that you SEPARATE them, leaving a gap between them that you can exploit with a subsequent shot. LIFT AND SEPARATE is a winning dinking strategy.

There are very few situations wherein hitting AT one of your opponents is the best tactic. Here are the only two that come readily to my mind.

1. One of your opponents is at his baseline. The other opponent is at the kitchen. You are at the kitchen. You are presented with a high shot you can easily slam. You might choose to slam it directly at your nearest opponent, believing that you can beat his reflexes.

2. One or both of your opponents are at the kitchen. You are at the kitchen too. You are presented with a shot that you want, or need, to slam. But the ball is a little bit too low to slam into your opponents' court. Again, you might choose to slam it directly at an opponent, using him as a backstop so that your shot can't go long.

If you can think of other tactical situations where hitting at an opponent is better than hitting around them I'd like to hear what they are.

Pickleball Pointers

All in all, I believe that the effectiveness of your shots will improve dramatically if you aim them around, not at, your opponents.

Ron

Section VI --- Tactics

LET IT GO!!!!!!!!!!!!!!!!!!!!!!!!!

What is the most difficult shot in pickleball to master?

Many players will tell you that it's the third shot drop. I agree that the third shot drop is a difficult shot to master.

But I think the most difficult shot is one you shouldn't take.
- --It's the shot that's going out of bounds, but you hit it anyway.
- --It's your opponent's high smash that you block back onto the court.
- --It's the lob that will surely be long or wide.

It's kind of embarrassing to let a ball go only to see it bounce in. No one wants to look like they are lazy or playing half-heartedly, so they hit balls that they should let go. But if you want to be a really good player, you'll have to learn to let shots go.

If your opponents know that you'll hit shots that are going out, they'll continue to hit those difficult to return shots. This is especially true of slammers. They will slam higher and harder as long as you don't punish them by letting their shots go out.

Certainly you'll have to block some of their slams – those that you believe will bounce in and those that would hit you. But all of their other slams, you must learn to let go. Letting them go will have two positive consequences for you. First, you'll win the rally. Second, you'll discourage them from slamming (which is probably their favorite tactic).

Your partner probably can't help you decide whether to return a slam. It happens too fast. You'll have to make that decision on your own.

But your partner should be able to help you on the decision regarding a lob over you.

If he KNOWS that the lob will be out, he can merely say NO or LET IT GO.
If he SUSPECTS that it will be out, he can say BOUNCE IT. If you let it bounce before you hit it, both of you will know for certain whether you need to return it.
On lobs over you, your job is to LISTEN to your partner and take his advice. Your partner's job is to COMMUNICATE his opinion to you.

Section VI --- Tactics

Sure, sometimes you'll let a ball go only to see it fall in. But if you guess right 51% of the time, you're ahead of the game.

Ron

AFTER A GREAT SAVE............

After a great save, I always redouble my efforts to win the rally. In particular, I make sure that I don't miss an easy shot.

If my partner makes a great save, I want him to know that his effort was worthwhile. There's nothing more discouraging than making a great save and then having your partner lose the rally by missing a setup.

If one of my opponents makes a great save, I don't want him to think his effort was worthwhile. I want to win the rally so that he believes he might as well not put forth the effort needed to make great saves in the future.

Ron

Section VI --- Tactics

WHAT'S YOUR TARGET?

It's important to envision a target for every shot you take. Hitting a shot without having a specific target well in mind is probably the leading cause of poorly placed shots. And the more precise the target, the more accurate your shot will be.

When envisioning a target, you have several choices. Your target could be a specific spot on one of your opponents. Or it could be a specific spot on the court between/around your opponents.

As you mentally select your target, (Yeah, I know that this must happen in fractions of a second. But it MUST happen.), you must let the nature of the shot determine the target. For example, if you decide to slam a shot that bounces to you fairly low, you probably want to mentally select a spot on one of your opponents' torsos so that the ball will hit your opponent rather than flying long.

A slam that you can take in the air, or that bounces high may be better targeted at one of your opponents' feet.

Pickleball Pointers

If you have room to hit a ball between or around your opponents, then your target should be a specific point on the court. Your peripheral vision will know where your opponents are, but your focused concentration must be the spot you want the ball to land while your vision is focused on the ball.

Oh, yeah, your actual vision must always be on the ball until it leaves your paddle. But your "mental vision" should be on the spot you want that ball to hit on the other side of the net.

Ron

Section VI --- Tactics

OFFENSE OR DEFENSE?

Should your team play offensively or defensively? First let's define "offensive" and "defensive".

For this discussion, an "offensive" team would be the team that prefers to hit the ball hard (slammers). And a "defensive" team is a team that typically doesn't hit the ball as hard as their opponents do.

I'd suggest that it doesn't really matter whether your team is typically offensive or defensive. What matters is whether you can force your opponents to play outside of their comfort zones --- to put them in situations where they make mistakes.

Remember the chapter entitled "The Chameleon"? You optimize your chance of winning when you force your opponents to hit their worst shots while you hit your best shots. "It's going to be my best shots against your worst shots all day long!!!!" If you can do that and your opponents still beat you, they deserve the win. Nothing you do guarantees a win. There are players you simply can't beat and games you can't win. But you maximize your chance of winning by preventing your opponents from using their best weapons against you.

Note that, at the beginning of a game, you may not know how to force your opponents into hitting their worst shots while they allow you to hit your best. That's why it's critical for you to keep an observant, open, flexible mind as the game progresses. Just keep trying various combinations until you identify your opponents' weaknesses. Then attack those weaknesses.

Ron

Section VI --- Tactics

TO LOB, OR NOT TO LOB,
THAT IS THE QUESTION

Each of us makes that decision every time we hit a shot. Pickleball coaches generally tell us that we lob too much --- that lobs aren't effective. I'd agree. I know that I lob too much. That's partly a hold-over from my tennis days where lobs were reasonably effective. And, it's partly because it's easy to lob. (It's just not easy to lob **effectively** in pickleball.) But I'd argue that there are times when a lob can be the best choice (or at least a reasonable choice). I'd suggest that there are three types of lobs and we need to consider each type separately.

THE OFFENSIVE LOB

The Offensive Lob is intended to win a point or at least put the opposition at a tactical disadvantage. The Offensive Lob must be hit from near the NVZ. And it should be hit when both opponents are at the NVZ. An example would be when all four players are dinking at the NVZ. Instead of a dink, hit an Offensive Lob. It is best hit with the element of surprise.

When properly executed, not only is the Offensive Lob highly effective, it is particularly demoralizing to your opponents. They've just lost a rally to a slow, soft shot that they could do absolutely nothing about. Now they become reluctant to come to the NVZ because they fear your lob.

To be most effective, the Offensive Lob should only be hit high enough to prevent the opponent from reaching it. If you hit it too high, your opponent may have time to retreat and smash an overhead back at you. (This is not a good thing!)

After hitting a good Offensive Lob, both you and your partner should get to the NVZ and prepare to put away a weak return.

THE DEFENSIVE LOB

The Defensive Lob may be an option when you are at a tactical disadvantage and need to buy time to regroup. If your opponent hits a good shot wide and you must move outside of the court to return it, you may need to hit a Defensive Lob to buy enough time to return to the court.

It is far better not to allow your opponents to put you in a position where a Defensive Lob is needed.

A Defensive Lob should be higher and deeper than an Offensive Lob. It should be high enough to allow you time to reposition yourself, and deep enough that your opponent can't slam it back from the NVZ. Note that there are nearly always other, alternative shots available to you. And they may be at least as effective as a Defensive Lob. As you move toward the shot you are planning to lob, your brain needs to mentally assess all of your alternatives and select the one you believe will be most effective. Don't just automatically hit a Defensive Lob every time you're in trouble.

After hitting a Defensive Lob, both you and your partner need to closely watch the lob and your opponents' reaction. If it's a "poor" lob and will probably be slammed back at you, both of you need to move as quickly as possible to the baseline and prepare to return a slam. If it's a "good" lob and it appears that your opponents will have difficulty returning it, or if they let it bounce, both of you should move to the NVZ and prepare to hit a winning shot.

THE DESPERATION LOB

As the name implies, this shot is made when your team is at such a tactical disadvantage that only a miracle could save you and no other shots are reasonably possible. Recognize that your odds of winning the point are very low, but hitting the Desperation Lob is better than just giving up on the shot. Hit the Desperation Lob as high and deep as you can (and still have a chance of it not being long.) Buy your team as much time as possible to regroup. Both of you should move as quickly as possible to the baseline and prepare to return a slam.

Ron

Section VI --- Tactics

PICK A PAIR

If you've watched many pickleball videos, you may have noticed that most of the matches shown on YouTube are of Pro and 5.0 players. Certainly those matches are interesting, entertaining, and informative. But I'm not sure that they are as instructive as some lower class matches might be.

Learning from the Pro and 5.0 matches is sort of like learning to drive by watching a Gran Prix road race. I'm not suggesting that Pro and 5.0 matches can't be instructive. However I think there is much to be learned by watching 3.5, 4.0 and 4.5 matches too. (I've never seen a match on You-Tube lower than 3.5.)

If you're a 3.0 player, your immediate goal should be to become a 3.5 (and then a 4.0) player. I'd suggest that watching 3.5 and 4.0 matches will teach you more about how to compete at those levels than will watching 5.0 or Pro matches.

As you watch matches, try to watch a variety of skill levels, not just the highest levels.

One good learning tool when you're watching lower-level matches is to focus on only one team. Pick a team at the start of the match. Study them as the match progresses. Determine how you would play against them. What are their strengths? And, more importantly, what are their weaknesses?

   ---Which of them is weaker?

   ---Does one, or both, of them fail to come to the NVZ aggressively?

   ---Does one, or both, of them have a weak backhand?

   ---Is one, or both, of them frequently out of position?

   ---Does one, or both, of them have difficulty dinking reliably?

   ---Does one, or both, of them have difficulty moving backward to handle lobs?

   ---Does one, or both, lack patience and will, therefore, hit low probability slams?

   ---Do they fail to move laterally as a team when one of them is drawn to the side of the court?

   ---What style of serve does each of them have difficulty returning?

   ---Do they fail to communicate and are thus often confused by shots between or over them?

   ---Do they have more difficulty with hard shots, deep shots, angled shots, or soft shots?

Section VI --- Tactics

What tactics would you employ against them?

Ron

IF YOU'RE DRAWN OFF THE COURT.......

A favorite strategy of my partners and me is to hit a wide, angled shot that draws one of our opponents out of position, preferably completely off the side of the court. Hitting that shot usually means that one of us can hit our opponent's return for a winner into the area the opponent has vacated to hit our angled shot.

That strategy is so effective that I began to worry about how to defend against it if our opponents used it on us.

Actually, being drawn off the court isn't a catastrophe. In fact, it isn't even necessarily a liability. There are several options to counter it. Those options depend on where you're drawn off.

AT THE NVZ

Here's a typical situation --- all four of you are at the net. You and the opponent diagonally across from you are in a dinking bout. He hits a dink that forces you wide off the court to return it.

You have three good options:

1. You can hit a low shot AROUND THE NET POST. Yep, it's legal. And if you hit it low, it's practically unreturnable. (Note that the further you have been drawn off the court, the easier this shot is to hit. Also note that this shot is only practical if you're at the NVZ. If you're further back, you probably can't get the angle needed.)

2. You can "redink" your opponent at an even greater angle, drawing him further off the court than you are. (If you choose this shot, your partner must slide to his sideline to prevent your opponent from hitting a winner around the net.)

3. You can hit an offensive lob into the nearest back corner. You'll actually be hitting around your nearest opponent, rather than over him.

BACK FROM THE NVZ

Here's a typical situation --- Your opponent serves to you. It's a wide angled serve, perhaps with spin, that draws you off the court to return it. Your choices are different than they were at the NVZ. Your angle won't be wide enough that you can hit an "around the net post" shot, so that's not an option. Because you are both wide off the court and back from the NVZ, you need to buy yourself some time to get back into position.

You have two good options:

1. You can hit a high shot back to the server at your opponents' baseline. (They just served, so both of your opponents are at their baseline.)

2. You can hit an angled shot of your own diagonally across the net. That should draw your opponent even further off the court than you are. This should give you time to recover and should give you or your partner an easy put-away in your opponent's open half-court.

The lesson here is that drawing your opponent off the court is an excellent strategy IF THEY DON'T KNOW HOW TO EFFECTIVELY RESPOND. But, being drawn off the court yourself doesn't necessarily constitute an adverse tactical position if you can execute the shots we've discussed above.

Ron

Section VI --- Tactics

IF YOU DO WHAT YOU ALWAYS DID.........

Did you ever notice that some players/teams get beaten by the same series of shots time after time?

They lose a rally and allow the next rally to progress through the same series of shots. Again and again they allow the rallies to be similar, until they eventually lose the match.

They never seem to consciously try to change the series of shots.

They never adapt.

There's a wise old saying that applies to them: "If you always do what you always did, you'll always get what you always got."

Don't be like those players. If you get beaten by a particular series of shots (especially if it happens twice or more), change your responses to their shots. Force the rally to evolve differently.

Pickleball Pointers

Conversely, if you win a rally, try to force subsequent rallies into the same sequence of shots.

Ron

Section VI --- Tactics

PREDICTABILITY

There is much power in being unpredictable. Conversely, being predictable is a serious weakness.

Imagine a major league pitcher who had only one type of pitch. Such a pitcher would not fare well against major league batters. Good pitchers have a variety of pitches. That variety makes them unpredictable. Their unpredictability makes them much more effective.

You can reduce your predictability by increasing the variety of your shots.

For every situation, I'd suggest that you develop at least two shots --- two serves, two returns, two third shots, etc. Using them both in a game will make you far less predictable.

I'm not a great player, so I need all the deception I can muster. In each game, I try to utilize three serves (lob, flat, and side spin), three returns (lob, flat, and short angle), three third shots (drop, hard down the middle, and lob), etc.

Pickleball Pointers

Practice one type of shot for each situation until you have it well mastered. Then set it aside for a while and practice another type of shot. When you have them both mastered and use them both in a game, you will see your effectiveness increase dramatically.

Ron

Section VI --- Tactics
THOUGHTS ON STACKING

Stacking is a strategy some teams use to gain a tactical advantage--- to take advantage of one teammate's strength or to protect a teammate's weakness.
Stacking involves the teammates switching sides of the court away from their normal orthodox sides before the start of a rally.

Some teams stack constantly. Other teams stack only in certain situations.

Stacking is made possible because, at the start of each rally, only the server is restricted regarding where he can stand. The other three players may legally stand anywhere, on or off the court, that they desire. This freedom allows the three players to start a rally in unorthodox positions which they believe to be advantageous.

As always, there are many good YouTube videos on stacking, including ones by Third Shot Sports and on Pickleball 411. (Have you gotten the feeling yet that YouTube is an invaluable resource?)

But stacking is not without its drawbacks.

Pickleball Pointers

If you and your partner forget your respective positions, you will lose a service turn or lose a point. If you stack, it's absolutely essential that both you and your partner know which of you is the correct server/receiver and which side of the court the server/receiver needs to be on.

If you are constantly on one side and your partner is constantly on the other side, your team's weakness will always be in the same locations. Once your opponents identify those weaknesses, they will always know where they are. It will be easy for them to attack your weaknesses.

If you and your partner use stacking to compensate for a weakness, you probably won't improve the weakness. In the long term, you'll be stunting your pickleball growth.

Third Shot Sports has a good video entitled "Defend Against Stackers".

I'd suggest that you try stacking just so you'll have a little experience with it. Then you and your partner can decide whether it is advantageous for you.

Ron

Section VI --- Tactics

<u>TIMEOUTS</u>

I've watched literally thousands of recreational games. In all of those games, I've never once seen a timeout taken for tactical reasons. I've seen timeouts to tie shoestrings, to change paddles, to get a drink of water, or to towel off, but never as a tactic. On the other hand, in many tournament games, I've seen timeouts used as a tactical weapon.

As a tactical weapon, it's usually used to interrupt an opponents' run of points.
If you watch high level tournament play, you'll notice that if one team scores three, or at most four, points in a row, the other team calls a timeout. That timeout has two purposes.

First, it can break the opponents' concentration. It can interrupt a negative (for you) flow of the game. (It's just like calling a timeout to ice a basketball player before he shoots a critical free throw or a football kicker before a critical field goal.)
Second, it gives you and your partner time to assess the reasons for your opponents' success and to develop a strategy to counteract it.

So remember, timeouts are a valuable tool in your tournament tool box. You may not use them in recreational play, but don't forget about them if you want to win tournament matches.

Ron

SECTION VII --- EXTERNAL FACTORS

Pickleball Pointers

ASYMMETRICAL CONDITIONS

Environmental conditions can make the court asymmetrical. This is obviously true outdoors. Wind and sun can force you to play entirely different tactical games depending on which side of the court you are on.

Even though this is obviously true, you'd be surprised how many players fail to take advantage of, or compensate for, environmental conditions. If you take environmental conditions into account in your shot selection, you'll have a major advantage over your opponents.

Are your opponents forced to look into the sun when they look up? If so, lob 'em to death.
(NOTE: If you don't wear a cap or visor, you are destined to lose whenever you play against smart players who have the "up-sun" side of the court.)

Are your opponents on the downwind side of the court? High, deep serves will push them back far beyond the base line. It should be easy to keep them deep with shots at their feet, preventing them from reaching the NVZ.

Section VII --- External Factors

Are your opponents on the upwind side of the court? Dinks and drop shots will die before your opponents can reach them.

Is there a crosswind? Lobs hit toward the upwind side of the court will drift sideways so much that they are very difficult to return. Angled shots that force your opponents to hit shots along the downwind side of the court will bring them many misses.

Just remember that adverse environmental conditions (particularly wind) may mean that your shot selection should be more conservative than normal.
Don't go for lines and corners, especially on the downwind side. Play safe shots and let your opponents make the environmentally-caused mistakes.

Asymmetrical environmental conditions also exist indoors. Recently I played in a tournament where the outside walls of the facility were covered by dark blue tarps. When I stood on the side of the court facing the walls, the ball was very easy to see. When I stood on the side of the court next to the tarp, the visual background was a tennis net and, beyond that, another pickleball court with folks playing on it ---- lots of color variations and movement which often made it difficult to see the ball.

Before each game, players flipped a coin. Winner got choice of serve or side. If I won, I chose the side facing the tarp. Every time my opponents won the toss, they chose service so I still got to choose side of the court. Side of the court was much more advantageous than who served first. My team got to look at the tarp every game we played.

Ron

Section VII --- External Factors

THE ENEMY OF MY ENEMY IS MY FRIEND

There's an ancient proverb that says "The Enemy of My Enemy Is My Friend". That's how I feel about difficult playing conditions, particularly the wind.

The wind isn't naturally a friend of mine. But many players consider the wind to be their enemy. And those players are my "enemies" (i.e. my competitors). That makes the wind my friend.

Admittedly, it's an uneasy friendship at best. The wind tries to beat me just like it tries to beat my competitors. But I've found ways to make her less of an enemy to me. In fact, I look forward to windy days.

What I'm going to share with you is applicable to all adverse environmental conditions. The wind seems to be particularly annoying to many players, so let's use it as an example.

There are two aspects to making the wind your friend----psychological and technical. In order to make the wind your friend, you must master both aspects.

PSYCHOLOGICAL ASPECTS OF PLAYING IN THE WIND

Let's tackle the psychological aspects first. How you feel emotionally about the wind can have a major impact on your play.

Most players would agree that negative emotions can adversely affect your game. Then you'll get discouraged and fail to play as well as you could. Before and during the match, it's best to remain completely stoic. There will be plenty of time for celebration or mourning after the last point is made. So let's talk a little about how to put yourself in the proper frame of mind, both before and during the match.

Before The Match, you should consciously remind yourself that:
1. The wind is just as bad for everyone else as it is for you. The wind does not put you at any disadvantage. It is only a disadvantage for players who allow it to psychologically bother them.
2. You shouldn't expect to play your personal best. It would be unrealistic to expect to play your best under adverse weather

Section VII --- External Factors

conditions. Any time you play (particularly in the wind) it is very important to have realistic expectations.

The wind will probably lower the level of your play. But it will lower the level of EVERYONE'S play. Once again, wind is not a disadvantage for you.

If you merely accept these truths, you'll already have an advantage over most players before the match even starts.

During The Match, you must:

    1. Trust your skills. Recognize that it is the wind, not a degradation in your skills that causes some missed shots.

    2. Refuse to worry about previous missed shots. Just calmly learn from them and move on.

    3. Remain emotionally detached. Stoicism will prevent your emotions from causing you to become demoralized. Remain calm.

    4. Focus totally on execution of the current shot. Any emotion (either positive or negative) can cause you to lose focus.

Accepting the conditions, refusing to become emotionally involved, and maintaining the correct goal will take you halfway to making the wind your friend.

Pickleball Pointers

TECHNICAL ASPECTS OF PLAYING IN THE WIND

From a technical standpoint, the most basic rule for playing in the wind is simple. Merely take more conservative shots than you normally would. Let your opponents miss the high risk shots.

Given an opportunity, if there's a crosswind, hit to the upwind side of the court where the wind will carry your shots into the court rather than the downwind side where the wind will carry them out.

You may also find it wise to hit shots lower and harder than you normally do. Low, hard shots will be less affected by the wind than high, soft shots.

Be very careful of gusty conditions. It's difficult enough to play in steady winds. Gusty winds multiply the problems. It won't be enough to just remember that you're on the downwind side of the court so you must hit the ball harder. You'll have to be aware of the wind conditions the instant before you hit each shot. And you'll have to include the wind in your evaluation of whether an opponent's shot is going to land in or out.

Ron

SECTION VIII --- SINGLES STRATEGY

Pickleball Pointers

SINGLES VERSUS DOUBLES STRATEGY

Many aspects of Singles pickleball mirror Doubles pickleball play. The paddles and balls are the same. The court is the same size (unlike tennis). The net is the same height. The scoring is the same (except there is no server 1 and server 2).

The physical aspects of play are the same.

The mental aspects of play are the same.

The concepts are the same.

The Four Commandments are the same.

But, in Singles, the execution of those physical, mental, and conceptual aspects and the Four Commandments are somewhat different. In many ways, Singles is a much simpler game strategically than is Doubles. You don't have to worry about your opponent poaching. You don't have to worry about which opponent is stronger. You don't have to worry about whether you or your partner should take a shot. You don't have to worry about communicating with a partner. You don't have to worry about an opponent who's already at the net when you serve. You don't have to remember which of you is the correct server. Etc., etc.

Section VIII --- Singles Strategy

From a tactical standpoint, Singles pickleball (and singles tennis) seem analogous to checkers, whereas Doubles pickleball (and doubles tennis) are more akin to chess.

Mentally, you'll have fewer things to think about. But physically, you'll need to protect more court area.

Let's look at our Four Commandments and see if we can apply them to Singles.

I. MINIMIZE THY UNFORCED ERRORS

1. Don't miss routine shots.

2. Move quickly to get into position early to make shots. Then stop before you hit the ball. Avoid hitting shots while you are moving. That will make more shots routine.

This Commandment is obviously fully applicable to Singles.

II. HIE THEE TO THE NON VOLLEY ZONE

1. At the start of every rally, your first goal should be to hit shots that allow you and your partner to get safely to your NVZ.

2. Hitting high, deep shots will give you more time to get to your NVZ.

> 3. Once you get to the NVZ, there are only two reasons you should back up.
>
>   A. Your opponent hits a lob that you must go back to hit.
>
>   B. You or your partner hits such a poor lob that it will be smashed back at you.
>
> 4. If you do get driven back from your NVZ, hit shots that will allow you to regain your NVZ ASAP.

Getting to the Non Volley Zone is a valuable tactic in Singles. But, it's much more difficult to get there SAFELY and, once there, to protect the entire width of the court without a partner. To get there safely and win a rally from there, you really need to put your opponent in a particularly bad tactical position --- one from which he would have a very difficult time hitting a passing shot.

One of the best ways to accomplish this is to hit shots alternately to his two back corners. Make him run from corner to corner at his baseline. First, you will force him to hit shots while he is moving which will degrade the accuracy and power of his shots. Second, from a corner, his shot selection choices will be much more limited than if he is in the middle of the court.

In Singles you should be more patient about moving forward. You must watch closely for the correct tactical opportunity.

Section VIII --- Singles Strategy

III. DIRECT THY SHOTS TOWARD THY OPPONENTS FEET

1. As long as you keep your opponents back from their NVZ, it should be easy to hit balls at their feet. If your opponents get to their NVZ, you'll need to dink them.

This Commandment is applicable to Singles. But, because you only have one opponent you'll have many opportunities to hit balls away from your opponent rather than at him. In Singles, it's always important to focus on hitting to the open court. Focus on hitting away from your opponent. As a minimum, you'll make him move to get to the ball. With luck and some skill on your part, he won't get there.

IV. PLAY AS A TEAM WITH THY PARTNER

1. Communication is critical and it's easy. It's a very simple language with only five basic phrases------- Mine, Yours, Out, Bounce It, and Switch. It's amazing that 99% of players do far too little communicating.

2. Move up, back, and laterally together.

Because you don't have a partner, this Commandment doesn't seem like it should apply. I'd suggest that you need to focus and communicate mentally with yourself as much as you would with a partner in Doubles. Don't become mentally lazy. Think to yourself just as you would talk to your partner.

Watch a few Singles matches on YouTube. Compare the strategy and shot placement used in them to the strategy and shot placement used in Doubles. You'll easily see how you need to modify your Doubles game to play effective Singles.

If you go back and read all of the Pointers in this book, I think you'll find that nearly all of them are directly applicable to Singles, or with a little thought on your part, can be adapted to the Singles game.

Ron

THE END

Well, I guess that we've come to the end of the Pointers I have to share with you. I hope that my thoughts will benefit each of you whose goal is to improve your performance and enjoyment in this wonderful game of Pickleball.

As I mentioned in the Introduction, these Pointers originally began as a series of emails to my closest pickleball friends. By reading this book, you, too, have become one of my pickleball friends.

So I'll leave you with one last quote:
"Remember, I'm pullin" for you. We're all in this together." Red Green

Ron

Made in the USA
Middletown, DE
22 April 2019